FOR QUEEN AND COMMONWEALTH

The C section of the Elswick Battery was one of the many permanent and volunteer artillery units from the Australian colonies that served in South Africa during the Boer War, 1899-1902. Australia had become a Commonwealth of states by the time the fighting was over, and in little more than a year such Boer War units would form Australia's regular artillery.

Australia
1788-1988

AUSTRALIANS AT WAR

FOR QUEEN AND COMMONWEALTH

KIT DENTON

TIME-LIFE BOOKS. AUSTRALIA
in association with JOHN FERGUSON. SYDNEY

Designed and produced by
John Ferguson Pty Ltd
100 Kippax Street,
Surry Hills, NSW 2010

Editor-in-Chief: John Ferguson
Consulting Editor: George C. Daniels
Series Director: Lesley McKay
Text Editor: Tony Love
Designer: Jane Tenney
Staff Writers: Deirdre McGarry, Julian Leatherdale
Picture Researcher: Elisa Clarke
Production Manager: Phillipa Denton
Assembly Artist: Josie Howlett

Time-Life Books, South Pacific Books Division
Managing Director: Bonita L. Boezeman
Production Manager: Ken G. Hiley

The Author: KIT DENTON is a freelance writer with a special interest in military history. His own military service was spent in the Royal Artillery and the Parachute Regiment followed by a spell with British Forces Network radio. After coming to Australia in 1950, he worked for 15 years in radio, mainly with the ABC, then as a freelance writer in film, radio and television. Of his six published books, the best known is *The Breaker*, the story of Breaker Morant. He has also written *Gallipoli — One Long Grave,* another in this series.

First published in 1987 by
Time-Life Books (Australia) Pty Ltd
15 Blue Street
North Sydney, NSW 2060.

© Time-Life Books (Australia) Pty Ltd 1987

This book is copyright. Apart from any fair dealing for the purposes of private study, research, criticism or review, as permitted under the Copyright Act, no part may be reproduced by any process without written permission. Inquiries should be addressed to the publisher.

National Library of Australia
cataloguing-in-publication data

Denton, Kit
For Queen and Commonwealth

   Bibliography.
   Includes index.
   ISBN 0 949118 08 7.
   1. South African War, 1899-1902 — Participation, Australian. 2. Australia — History, Military 3. China — History — Boxer Rebellion, 1899-1901 — Participation, Australian. 4. New Zealand — History — 1843-1870. 5. Sudan — History — 1862-1899.
   I Title. (Series: Australians at War; 5).
994

This publication has been partially funded by the Australian Bicentennial Authority as part of its programme to help celebrate Australia's Bicentennial in 1988.

Printed in Hong Kong.

CONTENTS

Picture Essay		From British Beginnings	6
Chapter	**1**	**Under the Southern Cross**	**14**
		Sword and Brush	33
	2	**Africa at Arms**	**42**
		Sudan Expedition	54
	3	**A Sailor's Campaign**	**60**
		The Elusive Boer	76
	4	**The Trek to War**	**86**
		Life on the Veldt	108
	5	**Roberts Takes the Reins**	**118**
		From Redcoat to Khaki	145
	6	**Endgame**	**154**

Bibliography 164
Acknowledgements 165
Picture Credits 165
Index 166

FROM BRITISH BEGINNINGS

Crowds cheer the march past of the NSW regiments in Sydney's Domain, there to celebrate Queen Victoria's birthday. (Samuel Gill, 1856.)

"This country will prove the most valuable acquisition Great Britain ever made."

POLICING THE COLONIES

In the first 80 years of settlement in Australia, the colonies' defence and internal law and order were in the hands of soldiers from Britain, although Australian-born youths were recruited into the ranks of the British Army as early as 1800. In addition, militia units on a government stipend and unpaid volunteers were raised from the civilian population for particular emergencies, such as the hunting down of bushrangers or suppressing convict rebellions. And throughout the 19th century, colonial governments in Australia formed volunteer infantry and artillery groups in response to the overseas needs of the British Empire.

The duties of the British solider in Australia in those early decades were largely of a policing and ceremonial nature. Troops guarded convict chain-gangs working on roads, supported settlers when they faced Aborigines and bushrangers, attended executions, assisted at large fires, supplied mounted escorts for gold in transit, and provided guards for goldfields, treasuries, gaols, quarantine stations and government houses. Emergency actions included putting down the goldminers' rebellion at the Eureka Stockade at Ballarat, in 1854; and in 1861 they helped the NSW Government during racial riots on the goldfields at Lambing Flats.

Despite the fear and hatred British troopers inspired in the Aborigine, the outlaw, the republican and the rebel goldminer, they symbolised for most loyal colonial civilians the protective and resplendent might of the British Empire. On State occasions, massed troops provided a glorious spectacle, firing artillery salutes or displaying military manouevres. The strains of the regimental band in Sydney's Domain, or the clattering hooves of the gold escort outside the Treasury, were familiar and reassuring sounds in the Australian colonies.

But Britain's units were eventually disbanded, and it was in 1870, when all British troops withdrew from Australia, that the colonies first faced the task of raising and funding a standing army of regular troops and co-ordinating a defence policy of their own. With such a move, and its added responsibilities, Australia took a step closer to its own nationhood.

Above: Escorted by mounted troopers, the first consignment of gold to arrive from Bathurst's goldfields settles to a halt outside the well-guarded Treasury buildings in Sydney on August 21, 1851. (Illustrated London News, 1852.) Left: Soldiers of the 11th North Devon Regiment of Foot engage in spectacular exercises with volunteer forces for a grand review and inspection of troops in Sydney. (Illustrated Sydney News, 1855.)

Colonial soldiers and police storm the Eureka Stockade at Ballarat on December 3, 1854, leaving 35 soldiers and civilians dead. (J.B. Henderson.)

Colonial troops provide a military escort for non-union labour during a shearing strike in Queensland in 1891. (Illustrated London News, 1891.)

1

UNDER THE SOUTHERN CROSS

Although by the mid-1800s Australia had begun to forge a separate identity to the Mother Country, when the need for arms arose to quell a Maori uprising in New Zealand, colonial soldiers flocked eagerly to join the Colours.

The time between the middle of the 19th century and the beginning of the 20th was a crucial period; a crossroads for the land of Australia as it sat newly known in the world.

In those days Britain, to a large extent, was the world: her empire stretched beyond Alexander's and outmarched the legions of Rome; her dominion held sway over more land and sea than anyone had conquered and held before; her navy was paramount, her army was everywhere; and commerce and the banks of the world were at her bidding. She was the pre-eminent power in the world and that status had come from keeping a trading structure fully protected by force of arms.

All that began to change in the last half of the 1800s for the nature and the needs of the armed protection were changing. Between the Crimean War in the 1850s and the start of the Great War in 1914, the whole nature of soldiering was transformed — except perhaps for the thinking of many generals. Experiment and invention spurred a seesawing arms race and out of it all came three especially significant factors: the manually operated machine guns of the 1860s were redesigned by Hiram Maxim to work automatically; the simple cattle-containing twist of

Black leather shako with white pom-pom. The brass badge bears the regimental number of the 58th (Rutlandshire) Regiment of Foot.

steel called barbed wire was taken to the battlefield; and railway lines now snaking across the world carried military men and materiel as easily as they carried civilians.

The Crimean War was on the uphill side of the change. The American Civil War was at its crest, and the Franco-Prussian War rode the downhill slope. By the time the Prussian army laid siege to Paris in 1870 its commanders had taken careful note of what had happened in America. They saw how troop trains had become commonplace and great cannon and bulk supplies were moved long distances at speed on internal railways. They had noted the patents taken out on shepherds' and cattle-herders' barbed wire. They had studied work done in Europe and America by inventive gun-makers, and they made their decision. They placed Maxim machine guns on their shopping list — Maxim automatic machine guns.

Britain's generals were not as far-sighted, unaware that the tiny fights she had been involved in as the 19th century approached its halfway mark would be the last of their kind. Asian, African and Indian skirmishes, short-range in gunnery and musketry terms often ended hand-to-hand with blood on the bayonets. And then, within three years, came the Crimean War and the Indian Mutiny, differing from those lesser battles only in the numbers involved.

The swing into the 20th century was marked by the Boer War, the first major war since the Crimean, and by then the waging of war had begun its most sweeping change. Tactically, strategically, in attitudes, style and logistics, war had been changed for ever by the three new weapons — the mad brilliance of the machine gun, the wicked wire, and the wheel on steel. And even then there were commanders who clung grimly to the Crimean style and, in the face of the new technology, fought at Gallipoli and on the Somme as though nothing new had been invented in the killing line.

As the 19th century reached its midpoint, Britain had soldiers deployed in India, Asia, Africa, Australia, New Zealand, South America, and a hundred small and isolated stations on islands and atolls, in enclaves and trading posts and toeholds scattered around the globe. At the halfway mark her Redcoats were fighting Kaffirs and Basutos in Africa; within two years they were at war in Burma and a year later they put the Punjabi Mahrattas of northern India to the sword and annexed their land. In the decade of the 1850s the British Army fought in Persia, in the Indian province of Oudh, in Natal and in China — that last a vicious war to gain control of the enormously lucrative trade in opium. Then Britain fought back bitterly and brutally against the Indian Mutiny.

During that same period Australia did not so much undergo change as explode into being. As a penal settlement the continent had been as remote from Europe as any distant star. As a burgeoning colony it depended still on bringing almost everything to its shores, from skilfully wrought machinery to the much cruder tool of convict labour. It was when gold was discovered that the frenzy followed: half-a-million hopefuls sailed for the goldfields, one in every 50 of the population of Britain, and they were joined by diggers and speculators from half the countries of the world. Keeping order in the wild surge of a gold-hungry migration between the ports and the diggings was a major task, especially as many police threw up their jobs to join the hunt and a number of soldiers deserted, shouldering pick and shovel instead of musket. The social fabric of the country was changing in the heat of the gold crucible: the enforced introduction of licences for mining led to the insurrection of miners at the Eureka Stockade in 1854; troops were called in, shots fired and 35 men, soldiers and civilians, died. Political confrontation had come to Australia, and had been met head-on by government and the Redcoats.

That appellation had rung round the world for almost two centuries — the Redcoats. In a variety of patterns, under a dozen different kinds of hat and helmet, above breeches, kilts and trews, the bright brick-red uniform coat with its coloured facings and white or buff cross-belts had been in the sight — and the

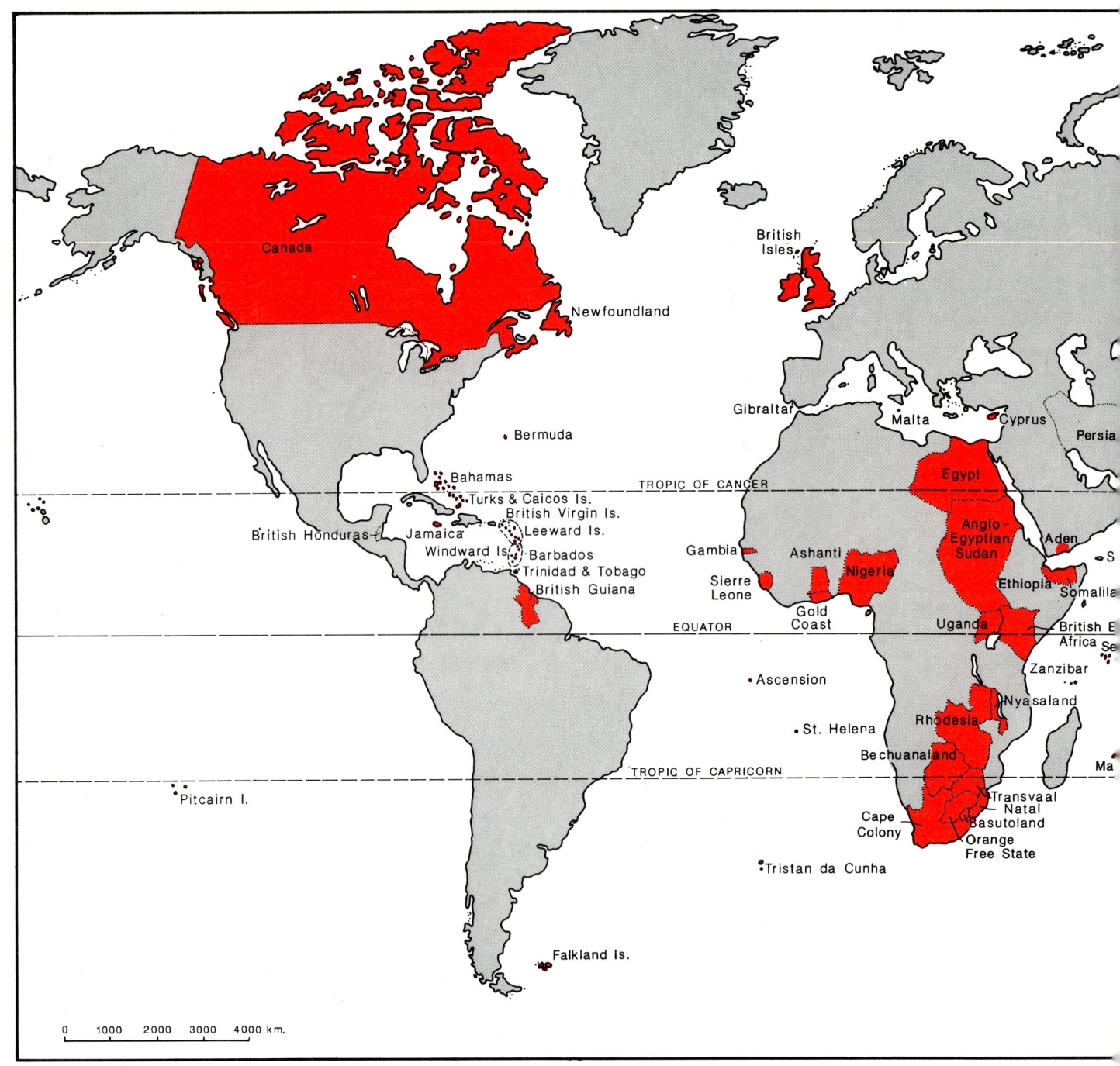

sights — of enemies from the deserts to the snows. Like the rest of the world as it spun towards the 20th century, Australia was seeing the last of the Redcoats, and the beginning of the end of the Mother Country's emotional grip.

That fierce clenching began to slacken, perhaps, with the first convicts to gain their freedom in Australia, legally or by escape. For them there were only two sides to society — authority and themselves. As more men and women were freed, as immigrants arrived, as the generations began to grow in the land, the feeling strengthened. There was the authority of London's establishment and its appointments, its decrees and soldiers, or the colony, which stood for something other than the old ways. There began to develop a new stance, a local argot, a perceptibly different attitude towards manners, morals and money. Even the stiffest of the local social codes allowed more free-and-easiness than would be the case in Britain and there was a general air of what came to be known as "larrikinism".

Yet, with it all, the emotional ties could not be so easily broken and in the 50 years to the new century, Britain had no need to call. When there were arms to be borne for the Mother Country,

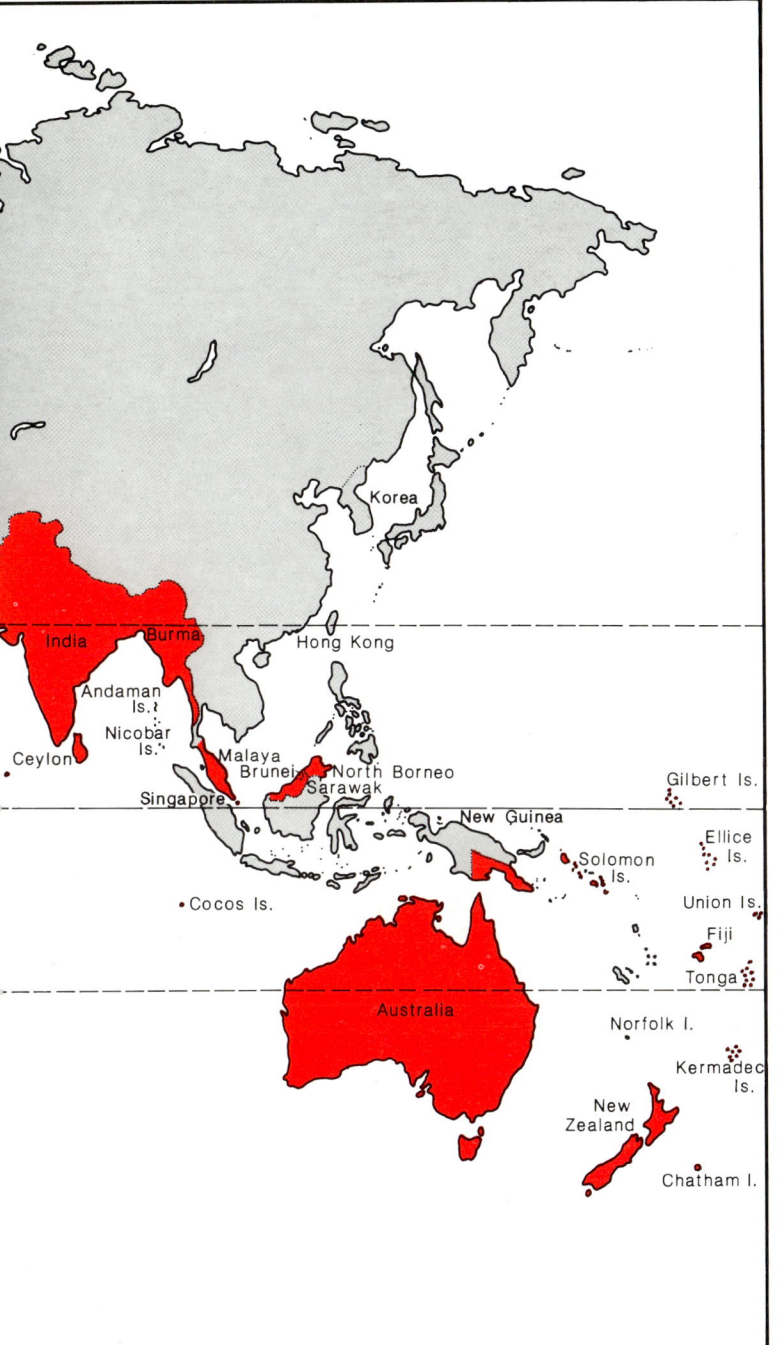

BRITISH MILITARY ACTIONS FROM 1845 TO 1902

AUSTRALIAN INVOLVEMENT MARKED*

1845	First Maori War, New Zealand*
	Anglo-Sikh War, India
1848	Second Sikh War
1849	Annexation of Punjab, India
1850	Anglo-Kaffir War and Basuto War, South Africa
1852	Burmese War
1853	Annexation of Mahratta State of Punjab
1854	Crimean War, Russia
1856	Anglo-Persian War
	Annexation of Oudh, India
	Takeover of Natal as a Crown colony, South Africa
	Anglo-Chinese War (Opium War)
1857	Indian Mutiny
1860	Second Maori War*
1868	Incursion into Ethiopia
1872	Annexation of Kimberley diamond fields, South Africa
1874	Ashanti War
	Annexation of Fiji Islands
1877	Kaffir War, South Africa
1879	Zulu War, South Africa
1881	First Boer War, South Africa
1882	Occupation of Cairo
1884	Sudanese War*
	Takes as protectorate North Bechuanaland, South Africa and South New Guinea; occupation of Port Hamilton in Korea
1888	Takes as protectorates Matabeleland, South Africa and Sarawak
1894	Takes as protectorate Uganda
1896	Matabele Revolt
1899	Second Boer War*
1900	Boxer Rebellion, China*

■ British Empire at its height, 1897

no matter where or why, the men of Australia would run cheering to the Colours. They did it as Redcoat regulars, as green- or grey-jacketed Rifle Volunteers, as blue-coated Gunners, as kilted crypto-Highlanders, in the Navy's blue and then, finally, in the sandy, dusty anonymity of khaki. It was then, as colonial Australians fighting the Boers, that they made some important discoveries. They found that as bushmen and horsemen they had things in common with their enemies which they did not have with their British kinsmen. They found that as soldiers they were, at least, the equals of the swaggering British Army. And they found that British officers, too often for safety, still acted as if they were leading the Redcoats.

In New Zealand, in the Sudan and in China, Australians had voluntarily taken up arms in Britain's cause and done it with bands and banners and the bravest of show. They did it again in South Africa, at the beginning, but by the end they had changed. Behind them was the colonial era, the time of the Redcoat, the age when Britain knew best. The century swung over and a sense of realism set in. Britain could be wrong, and had shown how in South Africa.

Loved and hated from afar, her Imperial Majesty Queen Victoria presided over the vast British Empire for 64 years.

The men from Australia who saw that happen were on the first of the three steps which would see them practically to the second half of the 20th century — and beyond. Step one took them to South Africa, while at home they saw the federation of the colonies into the Commonwealth of Australia. The second took them to Gallipoli, the Sinai and Palestine, and Europe, and bled them of a generation in the Great War. Step three took them to World War II and the American alliance.

What began in the mid-19th century with a man in a red uniform coat carrying a Brown Bess musket, ended at the start of the new century with a man in khaki carrying a magazine rifle and the bitter memories of a war which swung from fear to farce to firing party. At first he had a deep respect for his near-omnipotent Queen; in the end he was an independent man looking at the bejewelled Crown, thinking it might be just a little fancy for his taste.

The colonies which had sprung up and spread across Australia in the 19th century were no more than distant dominions of Her Majesty Queen Victoria. She held immediate regal sway over them all her long life as Queen, except in her last days. When she died on January 22, 1901, it was just three weeks after the day the British colonies in the far south had become a federation. Australia was now a Commonwealth, a place which would become the home of a nation.

When that happened there were thousands of Australia's sons in Africa, men who had volunteered to fight in the Mother Country's forces against the Boers. They had gone out of their homes as colonials and fought for more than a year as immediate subjects of the Crown. In 1901 Australian troops were raised by the newly-formed states; in 1902 by the Commonwealth; in both years the expense was met by the Imperial Government. Whether they were newly raised or seasoned veterans of the South African veldt, they became the first true Australian soldiers. But they were not the first volunteer soldiers to sail from Australia to fight in other lands.

Between the landing of Captain James Cook in 1770 and the end of the 19th century, the great sprawl of the continent of Australia was a temporary home for a quarter of the Line Regiments of the British Army. In the days when the Regiments of Foot were still sequentially numbered, 26 of them served in barracks, camps and garrisons under the Southern Cross: Royal Marines, Staff Corps, Royal Engineers and Royal Artillery, Irish, Scots, and Welsh men from both King's and Queen's Own Regiments, from the Highland Light Infantry, the City of Edinburgh, and from county regiments, many of them already old and honoured, from Devon, Kent and Somerset, from Middlesex, Dorset and Suffolk, from Northamptonshire, Leicestershire, Gloucestershire, Staffordshire, Yorkshire and from the smallest of the English counties, Rutlandshire.

The 58th (Rutlandshire) Regiment of Foot had been raised in 1755 and had won its first battle honours in Canada, fighting at the capture of Quebec where General Wolfe called them "the best trained battalion in America". They were part of Gibraltar's garrison during the 1779-1783 siege of the rock by Spain and they fought against Napoleon in Egypt and in the Peninsular War, and then in the American War in 1814. Beginning in 1843 the regiment was sent, a half-company at a time, to guard convicts being shipped to the penal colony of New South Wales and then to take up garrison duty there. There were 1,118 of them at full muster, from Lieutenant-Colonel R. H. Wynyard down to the smallest of the drummer lads. Every one of them was a regular, a minimum 15-year man, but many of them had served much longer; their Colonel had seen 28 years in the scarlet uniform with the sombre black facings which gave the regiment its nickname of the Black Cuffs.

On February 13, 1845, the 58th Regiment of Foot was ordered to provide a detachment to sail for Auckland, in New Zealand, and to place the entire command on standby. Captain H. Matson, an officer with 30 years' service, commanded the advance party. He marched the 110 men of No. 9 Company and some supplements from the regiment's Light Company of skirmishers down to Circular Quay to board the first available ships. The frigate HMS *North Star* and the transport *Velocity* took them, and on March 10, 1845, they sailed out of Sydney Harbour to win a new honour for the 58th of Foot. They were the first soldiers to leave Australia's shores on active service.

Awaiting them across the Tasman Sea was a very different kind of enemy from any they had known before. The Dutchman Abel Tasman was afraid of them. They attacked his ship in war canoes and killed four of his men, causing him to name the place where it happened Murderer's Bay. James Cook, when he first met them in 1769, wrote of them as "a brave and warlike people, with sentiments devoid of treachery." An Anglican missionary, Thomas Kendall, said, "I have been so poisoned by the apparent sublimity of their ideas, that I have been almost completely turned from a Christian to a heathen."

They were the Maoris of New Zealand, physically among the strongest people in the world and, in 1845, at war with the majesty and might of England's crown.

As with so much of Europe's expansion into the wider world, the flag followed trade. It was

THE QUEEN'S SHILLING

In the 18th and 19th centuries, it was the task of recruiting sergeants to go about the country, each accompanied, as a rule, by a drummer-boy and sometimes a fifer. When a likely recruit was found, the sergeant, on enlisting him, would pay him a shilling as his enrolment bounty. Once the shilling was taken, the young man was deemed in law to be a soldier. There were many occasions when a possible recruit was still expressing doubts and a common way to overcome them was for the recruiting sergeant to drop a shilling into a pot of beer and press it on the hesitant man. Even a sip at the beer was then construed as taking, or drinking, the King's Shilling. In Victoria's day, of course, it was known as the Queen's Shilling.

Confident of success, two recruitment officers lure a youth into army life.

British negotiator Captain Hobson (seated centre at table) watches respected Maori chief Tamati Waka Nene sign the Treaty of Waitangi on February 6, 1840.

Abel Tasman who named the islands *Nieuw Zeeland* after the province of Zeeland in the Netherlands, but his discovery in 1642 was kept secret. His employers, the Dutch East India Company, could see a healthy trading potential in the new lands and had no desire to let another nation into the secret. But by the time Cook rediscovered and charted the islands in 1769, the Dutch had done nothing about development or settlement. Between then and the century's end, the only sign of European growth was a small population of largely lawless men, deserters from whaling and sealing ships, the odd adventurer, and escaped convicts from the penal settlements of New South Wales and Norfolk Island.

With the publication of Cook's information about the place, British trade took an interest at once and the New Zealand Company, formed to colonise the islands, sent the first settlers out across the world in 1839. In doing so, they virtually forced the British Government to claim the country for the crown. A naval officer, Captain William Hobson, was sent to negotiate with the Maoris the prospect of Britain annexing their country, a country whose European population was then about 2,000, mostly "disagreeables" as Hobson called them. One of the New Zealand Company's settlers wrote in a letter back to England, "Everyone does as he likes except when his neighbours will not let him," and the Maoris, still innocent, were the victims of unscrupulous land sharks and traders.

Hobson met several hundred Maori chiefs at Waitangi on the North Island on February 5, 1840. Aptly, in the light of what was to follow, the name means "The Waters of Lamentation". Many of the chiefs had no desire to agree to annexation, but one of their number, a passionate speaker as well as an established warrior, Tamati Waka Nene, won them over.

He imposed conditions on Hobson, saying: "You must preserve our customs and never permit our lands to be wrested from us. Stay then our friend, our father, our Governor." Fifty chiefs signed the Treaty of Waitangi and 500 more in the days which followed. They were guaranteed possession of their lands and all the rights of British subjects.

All this took place on the North Island; Hobson made no attempt to deal with the southern tribes. On May 21, 1840, he made the formal act of annexation of the entire country and New Zealand became another pink patch on the map of the Empire. Five years later, the pink became blood-red.

Maiki Hill stood above the few scattered buildings of Kororareka, looking out on the calm beauty of the Bay of Islands in the far north of New Zealand. On March 11, 1845, it was the most northerly outpost of British colonisation of the land; there were a few settlers and traders, some with families, the sailors and Royal Marines from the half-dozen ships in the bay and a small detachment of soldiers of the 96th Regiment of Foot.

The settlers and soldiers lived in a rough wooden barracks inside a stockade of tree-trunks and they, the Marines, and sailors of the naval sloop HMS *Hazard,* manned the old ships' guns which were the settlement's defences. There were four guns in all, three in a small blockhouse and one in a redoubt covering the entrance to the little township. Above them, on the top of Maiki Hill, a picquet-guard, the sentries, were mounted round the tall flagstaff from which flew the symbol of British sovereignty, the Union Flag.

The flagstaff had been attacked and cut down three times before and each time the attackers had been run off and the staff re-erected. Those earlier attacks had been part of the Maori reaction to the signing of the Treaty of Waitangi. Despite its terms, despite the promises made, there were many *pakeha* — white men — who were only too anxious to steal from and exploit the Maori, and to take his land.

All tribal lands were held in common — a fact which the treaty had not considered — and even the Maoris who had supported the signing of the treaty, even the ones who had converted to Christianity, could not break the Maori code of conduct, the *tapu,* and sell land individually. The conflicts set up within the Maoris and between them and the whites could only lead to trouble, and given the nature of the Maoris, the trouble could only be active and warlike.

There had been small fights and killings over land surveys; there had been social changes among and within the tribes as the settlers brought in new ideas, new products, new desires for European goods. And, as the settlers began to congregate in Auckland and make it a town and an import centre, the tribes were forced to deal more and more with the townspeople and their governing authority. For many of them this was no hardship, but for a great many others the British settlers and everything they brought in their train were hated and to be destroyed. Numerically, the odds were in favour of the Maoris. There were more than 65,000 of them in the North Island alone and less than 1,000 British troops, including the Royal Marine detachments aboard naval vessels. Numbers aside, the very strong, very belligerent Maoris, fighting on their own ground, were a frightening enemy even for seasoned troops.

On this morning of March 11, 1845, the hillside above Kororareka was suddenly alive with leaping, yelling figures, too many and too ferocious for the small picquet-guard, who died where they stood. The flagstaff was hacked down across their bodies, and the flag torn and trampled underfoot. The Maori leader, Hone Heke Pokai, a noted chief and warrior, could see from the hill that his men were already into the houses and stores below, and that there was a fierce little battle raging between his burly tattooed warriors and the mixed force of the settlement, men in uniform and civilians alike. There were less than a hundred of them all told, but they managed to form a shield wall and to get the women and children away in boats to the

Chief Hone Heke grips a captured musket like a warrior's spear. His rebel army resisted the British until January 1846.

The last of the garrison withdrew and the small flotilla of ships pulled away, bound for Auckland. They left 19 of their company dead on Maiki Hill and in Kororareka. Some people called it the battle of Flagstaff Hill. No one recognised it as the first real action in a quarter of a century of war.

The first detachment of the 58th of Foot, the Black Cuffs, were a day out to sea when Hone Heke's attack against the flagstaff went in. Thirteen days later, on March 24, they went ashore at an Auckland stunned and frightened by the events of Kororareka and were almost at once put to guard outlying sectors of the growing town. The Governor had already sent off an urgent request to Australia for more military help and, back in Sydney, Major Cyprian Bridge, acting in command of the 58th, received his orders "to embark on the shortest notice for New Zealand on special service."

Captain Russell's Company sailed on April 8 for Wellington, where Maori tribes in the Hutt Valley were causing trouble. On April 10, Major Bridge embarked 212 all ranks for Auckland — the regiment's Grenadier Company, Captain Thompson's No. 3 Company and the band. The rest would follow as ships could be found for them. The inclusion of the bandsmen was no frivolous act; in combat they worked as stretcher-bearers and it seemed likely there would be some fighting.

Adverse winds kept the contingent at sea for 14 days until they put into Auckland on April 22, 1845. Five days later the 58th sailed again, leaving Captain Matson's No. 9 Company as a town garrison. The regiment, and a number of Auckland volunteers, had come under the command of Lieutenant-Colonel William Hulme, whose 96th Regiment was already stationed in New Zealand, and they headed north in three ships back to the Bay of Islands where there was a matter of honour to be avenged and British discipline to be imposed.

This expedition exposed all the salient points of the Maori wars which followed. The Crown forces, military, naval and civilian-volunteer,

ships in the bay, as well as holding off the wild Maoris, further inflamed by the store of rum they had found. The settlement was burning and near noon there was the sudden shock of the garrison's magazine exploding.

The commander of HMS *Hazard*, Lieutenant George Philpotts, ordered his guns to bear on the Maoris. The fall of shot added to the destruction although, oddly, neither the navy's guns nor the rampaging Maoris caused any damage to the two little churches in the settlement, one Anglican, the other Catholic. Hone Heke, like many other Maoris, had been converted to Christianity and had as great a respect for Christian temples and icons as for any of the old gods of his people.

Chief Tamati Waka Nene urged his peers to accept the gifts of British civilisation. He took up the spear for the Imperial forces.

fought well, often under very skilful command. The Maoris fought superbly, utterly without fear and under excellent commanders, and their knowledge of warfare, especially of entrenched fortifications, amazed professional British officers. But the Maoris were divided, many of them supporting the British, principal among them Tamati Waka Nene, nicknamed by the British soldiers "Timothy Walker". He was the chief who had spoken with passion in favour of the Treaty of Waitangi and who was steadfast in his loyalty to the Crown.

Land was at the bottom of all the fighting. The rights guaranteed to the Maoris at Waitangi were never fully granted; there was always the feeling among the tribes that they had received less than justice. Despite men like Tamati Waka and his followers, despite the many conversions to Christianity among the Maoris, there were to be four wars in 25 years because of that feeling. And the 58th (Rutlandshire) Regiment of Foot, when it went out of Australia and across the Tasman Ocean, cut the soldiering pattern for the men who followed. A considerable part of that pattern was the vivid tone of surprise as professional soldiers found that "rebellious natives" were — at the least — as good at the arts of war as any of the trained and uniformed men in the Queen's regiments.

On May 3, 1845, Colonel Hulme moved against the position which Hone Heke had fortified at Puketutu, on Lake Omapere. Apart from the 58th, Hulme was backed by a 9-pounder rocket battery and a contingent of Royal Marines and sailors from HMS *Hazard*. He had Tamati Waka with him, too, uncomfortably dressed in a presentation military uniform, complete with cocked hat and boots, all of which he swiftly shed as they moved forward. In lowering weather, then in rain, they marched for four days, their rations and ammunition soaked, unable to sleep properly at night without lying in deepening puddles. They were at last able to dry out at Tamati Waka's *pa,* his solidly defended village, sheltering first, then carrying out a reconnaissance the next day.

On the 8th, Hulme attacked Hone Heke's position. It was no simple task. The assault was to go in three storming parties, the 58th's Light Company, a mixed company from the 96th and the Royal Marines, and a party of sailors from HMS *Hazard.* Tamati Waka's men held guard on the left flank and Lake Omapere's swampy verge shielded the right. The attack began with a rocket bombardment and then the storming parties went in, taking casualties but reaching the breastworks and able to see to the stout palisades beyond. The Light Company opened fire from the rear. Chief Kawiti, Hone Heke's principal ally and a fine warrior, had lain hidden in a screen of light trees with a party of 300 men. As they rose, shouting their battle cries and making fierce grimaces, the 58th

Colonel Despard assembles his 600-strong force for a frontal assault on Chief Kawiti's Ohaeawai fortress. A smaller party attacks a nearby Maori hill post. (Bridge)

coolly faced about and met the rush with controlled volleyfire, followed by a charge, bayonets flickering wickedly among the Maoris. Kawiti's men broke and ran for the shelter of the ravine which ran alongside the *pa*.

The other two storming parties fought a bitter fight at and then over the breastworks and gradually pushed the Maoris back behind their palisade. But no one could go further. Both sides were exhausted: Hulme's rocket battery was out of ammunition and the Maori fortifications were too strong to be taken by musket and courage alone. Hulme withdrew his men to the discomforts of a bush camp and a meagre meal.

His little command had lost 14 killed and 38 wounded, almost half that total from the ranks of the 58th. And then rain came bucketing down that night to add to the general feeling of misery, not much relieved by the estimate that Hone Heke and his partner Kawiti had lost well over 100 warriors. The most that could be said was that the British had found the Maori warriors more than simple "rebellious natives".

The 58th were the first soldiers out of Australia to have shed blood overseas — their own and an enemy's — and they had learned some valuable lessons in their initial fight with the Maoris. Their commander, Major Cyprian Bridge, had learned the worth of Maori allies and enemies alike. He wrote: "I have no hesitation in asserting that mutual good feeling between the two races has been much increased by these proceedings; that each holds the other in greater respect and that a more kindly intercourse will be the consequence."

What the Maoris learned is doubtful. One of their accounts says, in part, "It was wrong of the soldiers to curse us. We were doing no harm. We were only fighting them."

On May 10, Hulme abandoned the attack on Hone Heke's *pa*, withdrew his force and pulled back to the sloop HMS *Hazard*. Major Bridge's pious hopes for "a more kindly intercourse" were not to be realised. Even after Maori warriors had drifted away to go home to their families, even without any of the tribal and inter-tribal unity Hone Heke had inspired, the fighting in that northern war burned on until the early spring of 1847. Among the tribes there were enough minor leaders to incite violence, and for many of the Maoris, to whom war was as much a religious game as a political or economic necessity, it was enough that there were *pakehas* to be fought. It was an uneasy time of mistrust, of ambush, and sporadic outbursts of violence. The flame of the fighting refused to die out completely and was still flickering in 1848, ready to blaze again.

Taranaki is the area of the North Island of New Zealand lying between Auckland, Wellington and the sea at New Plymouth. It is a lush, well-watered area and the Taranaki tribe of Maoris had long lived well there. That good life began to change for the worse with the influx of the *pakeha;* first the whalers in the early 1800s, then the settlers of the New Zealand Company. By 1845 there were more than 1,000 of them living on the rolling hills, on the ring-plain below Mount Egmont and along the many rain-fed streams which fed the Patea River in the south and the Waitara River in the north.

The word spread soon enough that the region was splendid farming land with rich volcanic soil and plenty of water, and there was a swelling tide of incomers, land-hungry settlers from distant England, from other parts of New Zealand and more and more from Australia. Sealers and whalers, adventurers and sailors had been moving south across the Tasman Sea for years and there was a considerable and growing Australian interest in the smaller colony. Indeed, one of Australia's most prominent men, William Charles Wentworth, explorer, property-owner and politician, made a determined but unsuccessful attempt to buy a huge tract of the South Island from the Maoris.

Government land-agents, the only people who, under the Treaty of Waitangi, could buy and sell Maori land, were unable to keep pace with the rush of demands; settlers made individual and illegal deals or simply took land as squatters. Inevitably, there were tensions, then disputes, then violence. Heads were broken, shots were fired, people were killed.

Many Maoris soon became discontented with the selling-off of tribal lands, partly because they began to realise that they were getting poor prices, but principally because they came to understand that they were losing birthright and the power of ownership. As subjects of the distant Queen, as citizens under the Treaty of Waitangi, they found also that they were paying taxes on the land they did not sell and that the trading balance was against them. The pressures of an increasing population pushed up the prices of the commodities to which the Maoris had quickly become accustomed, but their saleable crops were fetching less because the white settler-farmers were in that market too.

Faced with these threats the Maori tribal leaders met together in 1858 and elected a king: a man who had refused to sign the Treaty of Waitangi, but who had nonetheless maintained good relations with the British. He was the aged Waitako chief Potatau Te Wherowhero who was crowned as King Potatau I. His followers hoped that all Maoris would unite under his rule, a hope which was not realised in Potatau's lifetime; nor did it occur, when, after his death in 1860, his son was crowned as King Tawhiao.

The King Movement, as it became known, was never universal enough for it to be officially recognised or sanctioned, or for its demands for better land dealings to be met. Governor Thomas Gore-Browne refused to acknowledge the Maori kingdom when a deputation of chiefs went to meet him, so the angry King Tawhiao took his followers into an area of the Waikato which became known as "King Country". There they began occasional harrying attacks on outlying settlements and farms, perhaps to impress rather than to start any major conflict. But, in February 1860, open war broke out when Governor Gore-Browne sent his locally based British troops to Waitara to settle a major land dispute. A senior and much admired tribal leader, Wiremu Kingi, irreverently christened "William King" by the soldiers, but known as "The Peacemaker" for his moderation, decided to fight. For a savage year he led the combined Taranaki and Waitara warriors in a running war

Chief Wiremu Kingi. He rallied the Taranaki tribes to fight Governor Gore-Browne's troops in Feburary 1860.

against the *pakeha* until, in 1861, British troops and local militia laid siege to his heavily-fortified *pa* at Te Arei where, after bloody fighting, Kingi finally surrendered and signed a truce.

The peace, such as it was, lasted no more than two years. Gore-Browne's successor, Sir George Grey, was friendly enough towards the Maoris, but he, too, refused to recognise the King Movement and, when the attacks on settlers and outposts became more frequent, the Governor sent soldiers to put down the "rebels".

At the Colonial Office in London, dispatches from New Zealand had made it obvious that there was serious trouble brewing in that far colony and more troops would be needed to settle things down. Major-General Thomas Pratt, commanding the Imperial Forces in Australia, sent a strong contingent of his troops across the Tasman; the Government of the Colony of Victoria dispatched its entire navy, the 580-ton steam corvette, *Victoria*. And London sent Major-General Duncan Cameron, a tough soldier and a seasoned veteran of the Crimean War, who took command of the six British battalions by then in New Zealand.

With the local militia units that had been raised, they dealt with the first sporadic and largely isolated phases of Maori rebellion. Divided as they were by tribal differences, even by family feuds, the Maoris only gradually began to assume the proportions of a major menace. Indeed, the alliance of tribe with tribe inside the King Movement, and the resulting seriousness of the attacks mounted against the white population, did not come to a real head until mid-1863. The King Movement tribes, feeding on their anger, were ready for war and Major-General Duncan Cameron decided to take it to them and teach them a lesson.

In July 1863, he led a force of gunboats up the broad reaches of the Waikato River, their decks packed with militiamen in blue-bloused uniforms, some of them led by regular officers from Australia, and the old hands of the 12th Regiment of Foot, the Suffolk Regiment and the 14th, the West Yorkshires.

They made a brave enough start on July 17, when they tackled the Maori warriors head-on at a system of entrenchments they had built at Koheroa. Cameron led his men from the front, and they over-ran the fortifications with surprising ease and few casualties. Then, feeling successful, they moved on up-river to a little place known as Meremere. There they stopped. Duncan Cameron, well versed in the profession of arms, was a cautious man. He believed in having everything he needed before venturing into enemy territory to fight and, in this case, he felt he needed more suitable boats, more supplies, and more men. The waters upriver were less easy than the deep and broad lower reaches; and he knew that Rangariri, the "Angry Heavens", was not far ahead. The *pa* there was a massive example of Maori military fortification.

There was a narrow neck of land between the Waikato River and the Waikare Lake, and the warriors dug a ditch across it, fronted that with a parapet and strengthened the whole of the first line with a square redoubt, its ditches three metres deep, with a six-metre-high parapet. They ran a line of camouflaged rifle pits parallel with the river so that they could not be outflanked by a waterborne attack and they dug more rifle pits into a ridge 400 metres back so that they were covered from the rear. Cameron looked on all this fairly sourly. He was not the sort of general who threw his troops away in useless assaults, and he had become disillusioned to boot with the cause which had brought him to face this Maori fortress. It was his feeling that the white New Zealanders were a greedy and selfish lot of land-grabbers compared to the "chivalrous, brave, poetic and extraordinarily wily Maoris."

Between that first fine flush at Koheroa in mid-July and October of 1863, Cameron's men slowly and relentlessly edged forward towards Rangariri, the speed of advance governed by the arrival of boats and supplies and the clever and continuous delays imposed by the Maoris. At home in the land, very many of them equipped with firearms taken from dead or wounded troops, skilful at camouflage, and the swift, darting attack, they presented a constant threat to Cameron and his men. While the Maoris did not actually take many lives nor bring many men low with wounds, their unrelenting skirmishing was an exhausting strain on regular soldier and militiaman alike.

As Cameron was moving cautiously up river, heading for Rangariri, news of his campaign was spreading in the Australian colonies. A recruiting mission sent from New Zealand focused its attention on the Australian goldfields, where it hoped to find disappointed adventurers lured by the promise of eventual settlement on confiscated Maori land. A pattern was being cut. Young men in Australia pushed forward to fight overseas for Britain — and for their own future. Eighty men from Sydney were the first of the first; they sailed on the schooner *Kate* and docked in Auckland harbour on September 3, 1863. A week later *Star of India* tied up alongside and was followed in the next fortnight by three more ships carrying volunteers. By the time that initial inflow stopped, there were 1,475 volunteers out of Australia, the last of them going ashore on

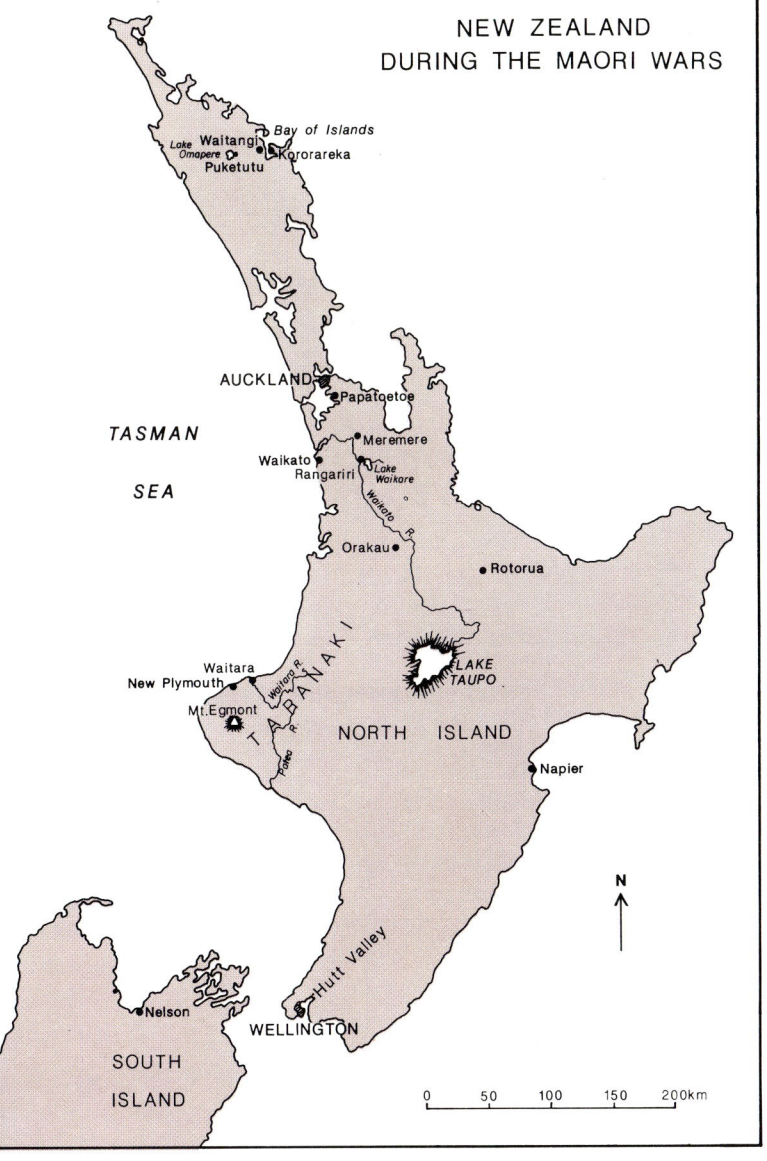

The North Island, home to militant Maori tribes but an attractive settlement for white colonists, became the battle zone for the Maori wars of the 1840s and 1860s. The fighting was ignited by native resentment of British land-grabbing.

September 25. In that week, the *Sydney Morning Herald*'s correspondent sent a dispatch reporting on fighting between Auckland and the Waikato "in which ten natives were killed and three encampments taken and destroyed, much plunder being also secured." The newcomers could be forgiven for wondering if they had come to a real war.

About halfway between Auckland and the massive *pa* at Rangariri was Papatoetoe, and there the Australian volunteers were taken into a formation with the Auckland Rifle Volunteers and a detachment from the Surrey Regiment, the 70th. The three units were formed into a flying column, working out of a redoubt and scouting and policing the hill country to the west where Maori warriors were active and scattered settlements endangered. The Australians were in the field and under fire, and took their first losses — two young lieutenants and a number of troops killed.

By the end of October, Cameron had worked out his plans to assault Rangariri. With the regulars now reinforced by increasing numbers of volunteers, he was able to maintain steady forward pressure, build up his supplies and keep his lines of communication covered; the volunteers were especially useful for that task. He settled on November 20 as the day for the attack on the *pa*.

In the three weeks prior to that, the Australian and New Zealand volunteers had become a little more military in pattern. There were enough of them to form two units, each 1,000 strong: the 1st Waikato Militia Regiment, largely men from Melbourne; and the 2nd, made up of Sydneysiders and volunteers from Otago and Nelson, many of them Australians who had been working gold there.

The "Waikatos", as they were known, would eventually double in numbers and form a 3rd and 4th regiment from 1,200 further volunteers who crossed the Tasman to New Zealand; men who had been given handsome inducements to volunteer. Aside from the prospect of taking up land in New Zealand, a possibility which had certainly drawn some of the men, they were paid two-shillings-and-sixpence a day while away from Australia, whether campaigning or not. If they were at a recognised fighting front, there was an extra shilling a day. Their free rations included a gill of rum daily plus a pound-and-a-quarter of bread, a pound of meat, tea, coffee, sugar, salt and pepper.

And, of course, they were uniformed. The men wore a less flamboyant version of the officers' outfits, which one local reporter called, "jacket of fine scarlet cloth, tastefully trimmed with silver, over which is worn a handsome silver shoulder belt. The trousers are tight steel grey with a stripe of silver lace on the side an inch and a half wide. The cap is grey with a silver band edged with scarlet. It is worn without peak but with an Indian puggaree." That was parade dress. In the field the militiamen wore simple soft forage caps, blue shirts and trousers, short boots and leggings.

Like campaigning soldiers everywhere, in every age, they grumbled. One of the Melbourne men wrote home, "We are having dreadful weather here, only now and then a few hours' sunshine, not enough to dry our beds. The bread we have is not fit for human food so we have refused it and commenced buying our own."

Neither did the free-and-easy Australians take kindly to the British Army's way of doing things — a clear foretaste of attitudes in later wars. A New Zealand volunteer, John Featon, wrote a book on the war in the Waikato, and in one chapter remarked of the Australians, "Many of them got into serious trouble for disobedience of orders, and found themselves in military cells minus their thick crop of curly black or brown hair, looking more like convicts than gentlemen-volunteers."

There was even trouble between the Australians and friendly and loyal Maoris. The New Zealand correspondent of the Melbourne *Argus* wrote in January 1864: "The Maoris, having found out that there is a distinction between the militiamen and the regulars, look down on the former, and the Waikatos have very lax ideas of the vested rights of friendly natives in property of any kind." Australians in uniform were already establishing a reputation for a degree of larrikinism.

At Rangariri, the Waikato River foamed at the bows of HMS *Avon* and HMS *Pioneer,* gunboats each towing a pair of armoured boats carrying supplies, ammunition and 320 men from the 40th Regiment, the Somersetshires, as reinforcements. They were sniped at for the last four or five kilometres. Then there was some trouble when *Pioneer* lost steerageway and ran aground a little below the appointed place, but the troops got ashore in good time. Cameron had decreed that the battle would start at four o'clock and, exactly on time, the General's two Armstrong guns — breech-loading, 12-pounder field-guns — opened fire, supported by the two gunboats which were anchored mid-stream.

Cameron had 1,200 men in his assault force and, after an hour of the artillery barrage, he moved them forward and out, skirmishers wide to the flanks and the soldiers the Maoris called "the red tribe" in the broad centre. Behind came the reserves, a party of pioneers — the forerunners of the modern era's engineers — with scaling ladders, the regimental surgeons and the bandsmen-cum-stretcher-bearers. No one appeared to pay much attention to the warriors, who had dodged and darted from the *pa* during the barrage and spread into the long scrub, each of them with a rifle.

The regiments moved forward, heralding their advance with the sort of growling scream of a cheer with which a charge so often began. But there was no charge. Ahead of them was close to 400 metres of country covered with ti-tree scrub, and the advance was a pushing walk, rifles at the high port, bayonets a-glint in the late afternoon sun. The Maoris hidden in the scrub opened fire. The soldiers of the three regiments, the Suffolks, the West Yorkshires and their

Men of the Hobart Town Volunteer Artillery and the First Tasmanian Rifles await the Empire's call in 1863.

General Duncan Cameron's troops (left) charge into a deep entrenchment and, under heavy fire, scramble up the steep parapet of the Rangariri pa. Maori riflemen surrendered the next day. (Charles Heaphy)

North Yorkshire companions, made good targets and they fell thickly in the bush, yet still pushed on.

As they reached the Maori parapet, the Somersetshire Regiment reinforcements were following hard behind them, but even with their help, the parapet could not be taken. The Maori fire from behind it, and enfilade of the troops from the flank and rear was too hot. The few hand-to-hand fights on the parapet were indecisive and, as afternoon dimmed towards evening, the best the soldiers could do against such strong defence was swing to their right and take a flanking position. Casualties had been heavy, including a party of sailors who had fought bravely, but had lost their commander, both their lieutenants and half their number struck down.

With nightfall, the action ended, the most advanced party of British troops sheltering in a deep ditch, part of which had been the Maoris' outer entrenchments. Although they were under sporadic, and heavy, fire throughout the night, they dug through the soft earth towards the *pa*, planning to blow the parapet in daylight. They were saved the trouble.

In the first clear dawning, the *pa* surrendered. The Maori losses were no heavier than those of their attackers, but they were out of ammunition and had held out only long enough to be sure that their leaders, King Towhai and Wiremu Tamihana, had got away with the bulk of the warriors. Some swam out while the first attack was being made; the rest took quickly to canoes along the river, heading upstream. There were almost 200 Maori prisoners taken out of a probable 1,000 who had been in and around the *pa* when the battle began. But there were 41 dead warriors and 42 British soldiers and sailors killed. Cameron's satisfaction at clearing the *pa* was diminished by those deaths.

There were more deaths and woundings in the wide country behind the action at Rangarari, in the rolling hills and the riverlands where the Australian volunteers were engaged in the sort of work which would, in a later century, become known as a police action. Lieutenants John Perceval and Thomas Norman, and several of their men from Melbourne fell in a brisk and savage little fight at Titi Hill on October 23, killed by bullet strike or greenstone battle-axe. They were, arguably, Australia's first war dead.

Aside from the New South Welshmen and Victorians who had become part of the Waikato regiments, there were Australians serving with the more exotically named Forest Rangers. These were specialist companies, led by Captain William Jackson and Captain Gustavus Von Tempsky, who operated in the bush as guerrillas, uniformed in rough, country-matching clothes and capable of swift and sudden attacks. The Australians who served with the Forest Rangers were good recruits for that kind of informal work, and they were involved in what was to be the final flourish in the Waikato war.

Von Tempsky's men and the Auckland Rifle Volunteers were spread thinly across the arc of country around Orakau, small scouting parties and fighting patrols active in the hunt for the Waikato chief, Rewi, who was strengthening a *pa* in the area and readying his warriors for a great battle. Through February 1864, bitter little fights were fought in the ti-tree scrub and the thick grass of the Waikato as the field commander, Brigadier-General Carey, moved his forces into position. Late on March 30, he pushed his troops forward: the regulars of the 40th and the 65th, the Forest Rangers, two field-gun detachments, 600 men from several regiments, including a company of the Victorians from the 1st Waikato, and detachments from the other Australian Waikato regiments.

On the following morning of the 31st, the Maoris under Rewi again showed their strength in defence and their worth as fighting men. They clearly repulsed a strong attack by the 18th Regiment, the very experienced Royal Irish supported by Von Tempsky's Forest Rangers, tough men all. Two massed bayonet charges were made and each was beaten off so decisively that Carey pulled the battered soldiers back and decided to bombard the upperworks with his six-pounders, while digging a long sap forward.

The cannonading and rifle fire went on through two days and a night until, a little before noon on April 2, the sap was close enough to the Maori breastwork for short-fused grenades to be tossed over. A leader in the operation was a South Australian barrister, Captain Walter Herford, who had given up a lucrative practice and volunteered for the most active service he could find. He was a fine shot and spent hours at the end of the sap, sniping at any enemy head he could spot. It was during a break from that deadly work, when he was cutting down a fence post to use as a tent prop, that a Maori sharp-shooter evened the score. Herford was struck in the eye, the bullet passed into his skull and he died a little later.

General Cameron, who had come up earlier, but left Carey to run the fight, maintained his good feelings about the Maoris who, 300 strong, held the *pa* against greatly superior numbers

Captain Gustavus Von Tempsky, commander of Forest Rangers.

and fire-power. Chief Rewi refused to surrender. The Maori account quotes him as addressing his warriors and their families, saying, "It was we who sought this battle. Wherefore then should we retreat? Let us abide by the fortune of war. If we are to die, let us die in battle. If we are to live, let us survive on the field of battle."

One of the interpreters who took forward an offer of surrender was Major William Mair, and he reported in a later account, "The outwork in front of me was a sort of double rifle pit with the *pa* or redoubt behind it. The Maoris were in rows, the nearest only a few yards from me. I cannot forget the dust-stained faces, bloodshot eyes and shaggy heads. One man aimed steadily at me all the time. I said in Maori, 'Friends, listen! This is the word of the General. Great is his admiration of your bravery. Let the fighting cease. Come out so that your bodies may be saved.' In a few minutes the answer came in a clear, firm tone, 'Friend, I shall fight against you for ever and ever!' Then I said, 'That is well for you men, but it is not right that the women and children should die. Let them come out.' There was a short deliberation and another voice made answer, 'If the men die, the women and children must die also.' "

There was nothing further to be said in the face of such stubborn bravery. The Waikato regiments charged the *pa* once and again, while grenades were thrown from the sap, the six-pounders roared and volley fire poured in. The Maoris fell in scores, but the *pa* held until Rewi formed his last warriors into a shield ring, their women and children inside, and hacked and bludgeoned their way out through the British and Australian troops and escaped, battered, bloodied, few in number but undefeated.

It was the effective end of the Waikato war, yet there was still an uneasy decade of fighting to come in New Zealand. With the government decision to confiscate the land of Maori rebels, a second war broke out in the Taranaki district, this one still bloodier and more fanatical. It was spearheaded by a Maori sect calling themselves the Hau Haus, a minority which preached a savage mixture of Maori belligerence and Old Testament eye-for-an-eye revenge theology. As a movement it was sufficiently unpopular that many Maoris joined with government troops to put it down.

Across that period the Waikato regiments were posted around the country as garrisons for several redoubt positions. Many of the men took up land grants and, when the Waikatos went home to NSW and Victoria, there were many who stayed to live in New Zealand.

In all, 2,675 men volunteered themselves from Australia into the Waikato regiments. Few of them had the chance to wear those gay scarlet and silver dress uniforms as there were not many parades, nor ceremonial occasions. Most of the men were less involved in the set-piece battles than in skirmishing and patrolling and policing. They, and the gold-mining Australians who enlisted in New Zealand from around Otago and Nelson, played a significant part in the Maori wars. There were no accurate casualty figures, the best estimate being "a few", but there were some notable firsts, more clearly seen with the lapse of time.

It was the first time a body of soldiers from Australia went voluntarily to fight overseas in a cause not directly their own. It was the first time colonial Australians fought "rebellious natives", a phrase which was to raise odd echoes later, in South Africa. It was the first time those colonials had shown the effects of their less-restrained life when they came into contact with the stiff formality of the British Army. The first time, but certainly not the last. And it was the first time that Australians and New Zealanders fought side by side. Such an alliance would occur again; a union which would later produce the famous ANZACS.

In the closing phase of the 1st Maori War, the 58th Regiment encamp at Ruapekapeka, near the pa of Maoris who defected to the British side. (Major Cyprian Bridge.)

SWORD AND BRUSH

Brandishing canoe paddles and two European muskets, Maori fighters perform a war-dance outside their pa in preparation for battle. (G. F. Angas.)

A Europeanised view of a pa near Wanganui by J. A. Gilfillan. The small elevated storehouses preserved clothing and food from damp and vermin.

Clubs, axes, spears and a warning gong surround three warriors preparing for attack. (G. F. Angas.)

Maori women peel potatoes and weave baskets and long capes from flax. The carving on the central pillar represents Te Rangihaeata, a chieftain leader of the anti-colonial struggle. (G. F. Angas.)

SKETCHES OF MAORI LIFE

By the time the first white man discovered New Zealand in 1642, the Maoris had belonged to the Land of the Long White Cloud for three centuries and developed a complex, creative culture. The natives of the South Island remained dispersed and nomadic, but on the North Island an intricate tribal society had emerged. Large clans under a chief's authority enjoyed a rich communal life regulated by *tapu*, a system of customs and traditional rules. These tribal communities lived in highly decorated longhouses clustered inside a well defended compound — a *pa* — encircled by ditches and a tree-trunk palisade.

Tribes were fiercely territorial, and intertribal warfare was a way of life; so much so, that fighting was sensibly restricted to the summer months between planting and harvesting of their staple crop, the sweet potato. Every adult male in a tribe was a trained warrior and warfare was governed by elaborate rituals of gift exchange, war dances and chants. A large arsenal of deadly weapons included ornate, blunt-edged killing clubs, and razor-sharp knives. It was common practice to feast on slain enemies after battle, a cannibalistic ritual of victory as well as a supplement to the diet.

The sketches of Maori life by Sydney Parkinson, the artist on Captain Cook's first voyage of 1769, started a European artistic love affair with Maori culture, particularly the beautiful designs adorning tattooed bodies and faces, flaxen cloaks and capes, carved gables on huts, and figureheads on war canoes, sculptured adzes and weapons. Two early colonial artists, John Alexander Gilfillan and George French Angas sketched and painted studies of Maori life even as relations with *pakeha* (white man) soured.

THE SOLDIER ARTISTS

When the first Maori war broke out in 1845, there were plenty of artists on hand to vividly record the dramatic incidents of the campaign. Many professional soldiers were handy with the pen and brush, as officers received some sketching tuition as part of military training. Major Cyprian Bridge, commanding the 58th Regiment, left many deftly executed watercolours depicting episodes of the first Maori war. It is a wonder that these soldier-artists found time to sketch at all; Henry Mount Langton Atcherly, who served as colour-sergeant with the 1st Waikato Militia Regiment from 1863 to 1867, was involved in actions throughout the Waikato campaign "amounting in all to 14 times under fire." A watercolour of the attack on a Hauhau stronghold in 1867 is his best known work. Major-General Horatio Gordon Robley was a veteran of colonial wars all over the Empire, and painted many war scenes in the 1860s campaign. He eventually took a Maori bride and continued to sketch Maori masks and tattoos.

But the spirit of adventure and courage shared by these front-line artists is most colourfully expressed in the career of the eccentric Prussian traveller, artist, and veteran soldier, Gustavus Von Tempsky, in command of the "guerilla" detachment called the Forest Rangers. As bullets grazed the trees and struck the earth inches from his body, Von Tempsky would readjust his position to get the best view of the battle he was sketching. He won loyalty from his men and admiration from the enemy, who called him *manu-rau* ("many birds") for his Rangers' fleet-footed mobility. In September 1868, this charismatic commander was trapped in a Maori ambush and died dramatically, brandishing his sword aloft. Spared the indignity of being eaten by the victorious Hau Hau, Von Tempsky was cremated upon a pyre with the ceremony attending a great warrior's death. His own epitaph was in the last letter to his wife: "An honourable death on the battlefield is a gift of God compared with a slower death."

Von Tempsky (second from right) leads his Forest Ranger Brigade, accompanied by

friendly Maori warriors and scouts, in the British advance through Taranaki in January 1866. (Gustavus Von Tempsky.)

At Nukumara camp, exhausted troopers from Major-General Cameron's Imperial forces in the West Coast campaign, maintain sentry duty only days after beating back several Maori attacks. (Lieutenant-Colonel E. A. Williams.)

The 600-man reconnoitring column of the Waikato 1st Regiment surprise a Maori force at Te Ranga. (Atcherly.)

The strongly fortified pa of Chief Puketutu resisted a British assault in April 1845. By year's end, Puketutu had become an ally. (Bridge.)

Under heavy fire from rebel leader Tamaikowha's men high on the opposite bank, the infantry of the 1st Waikato Militia Regiment struggle across the Waimana River in a vain and costly attempt to capture the enemy position. (Captain Henry Atcherly.)

Von Tempsky's Forest Rangers, helped by McDonnell's native contingent, wait for a Maori onslaught. (Von Tempsky.)

His Forest Rangers trapped, Von Tempsky is struck fatally as he runs to aid a wounded soldier. (Kennet Watkins.)

Smoke rises from the vanquished Ruapekapeka pa, overrun by British troops on January 11, 1846. (Bridge.)

Angry and confused Maori prisoners hand in their weapons and sign a surrender notice at Te Pepo. (Horatio Robley.)

2

AFRICA AT ARMS

In the Sudan, the Whirling Dervishes were on the rampage. A NSW contingent went promptly to Britain's aid, but its unflagging patriotism was rewarded not with battle honours, only the heat and dust of the harshest desert.

While the last flames of the Maori uprisings flickered into the dark, there was a more savage swinging of the sword across the world in the north-east of Africa — in the Sudan, where Egypt held nominal control, bolstered by British administrators and military advisers.

It was a physically hostile terrain, called in ancient times the Kingdom of Kush. And it was hostile in other ways, as the home of the Dervishes, fierce fighters, easily roused to fanatic excesses in the name of their religion, Islam. In 1883, after years of unrest and sporadic outbursts against foreign control and "infidels" in general, the Dervishes found a burning glass for their passions, a human focus who concentrated their hatred of Egypt into the raging blaze of a *jihad*, a holy war. They called him Muhammed Ahmed of Dongola, or al-Mahdi, "he who is guided aright". He called himself, simply, the Guide.

Under his spell, the Dervishes commenced a slaughter. Almost 10,000 Egyptian troops, commanded by a former Indian Army officer, General William Hicks, were defeated and massacred at El Obeid in November 1883. The Mahdi's right-hand man, Osman Digna, also rode against Egypt's Red Sea ports and there, at

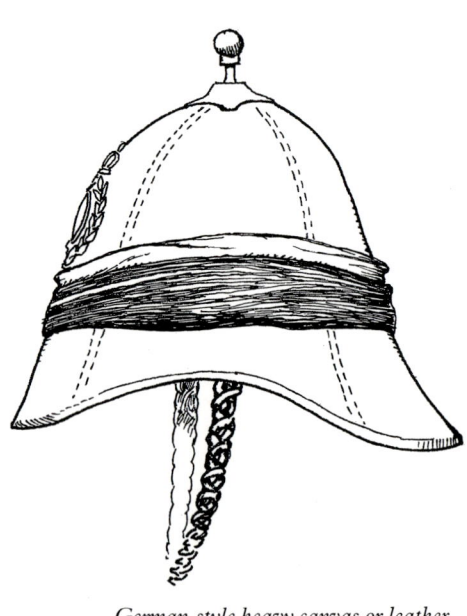

German-style heavy canvas or leather helmet, white for overseas service.

El Teb, near the port of Suakin in February 1884 wiped out another large Anglo-Egyptian force.

By then, something was being done to salvage the situation, though not, as might have been expected, in a military fashion. Britain had legislated against all forms of slavery within its Empire and, by what was seen as a logical extension, against slavery worldwide. Africa was an area in which Britain could hope to exercise great control with such measures, and it supported Egypt's control of the Sudan as part of an anti-slavery programme. With the Mahdi's forces running wild and two heavy defeats registered, there was strong pressure on Britain to act in defence of the Egyptians.

Prime Minister William Ewart Gladstone, unwilling to "indulge" in foreign enterprises or to incur the major expense involved in the commitment of troops, held out as long as he could, but was forced finally to take action — although he did it in the most limited way. He asked General Charles Gordon to undertake the task, virtually alone, and Gordon — mystic, humanist, martinet and fatalist — accepted. He left England on January 18, 1884, with orders to go to Khartoum, the Sudan's major city, to arrange the peaceful withdrawal of the Egyptians from the country to behind their own borders. Within days of his arrival, the city was under siege by the Mahdi's forces.

The river-moat guarding Khartoum's loopholed walls was Nile water, for the Blue and the White Niles met just beyond Khartoum. Within the walls there was a small garrison of Egyptian soldiers and almost 200,000 civilians. They looked to one man for their salvation, a British general who had made his name in China, an odd and introverted engineer known about the world as "Chinese" Gordon.

However, having arrived in Khartoum in February, Gordon seemed reluctant to abandon the city, and procrastinated in arranging the evacuation. By the end of the summer, there was no real chance that he could succeed in a mass withdrawal. The Mahdi's force tightened its grip, day by day for 317 long days. Food was at first scarce and then almost non-existent, the telegraph was cut, attacks were remorseless, and casualties and sickness were at plague proportions. With the advent of the dry season, the Nile waters began to drop and the moat's value as a major, outer defence evaporated little by little in the burning air beneath a brazen sky. It was a mark of Gordon's astonishing strength of purpose and his power to influence others that the siege lasted as long as it did.

In Britain, there was mounting rage at the way Gladstone delayed sending a relief column. The last telegraphed messages out of Khartoum had been amplified by Gordon's graphic journals which he had sent down the Nile by paddle-steamer, and their publication forced the Prime Minister into taking action; again slowly. A force was assembled in Egypt in August 1884, but it did not reach Khartoum for five terrible months, by which time the year had turned over and the relief was too late.

Two days before the rescuers marched into Khartoum, on January 26, 1885, the Mahdi's forces had broken the city's defences. They swarmed in thousands across the near-dry Nile moat, one party with a crude battering-ram making for a wooden doorway in the thickness of the wall. Hundreds of others ran against the walls with rickety ladders, scrambling up them, shrieking their battle-cries, ignoring the maimed and dead who fell past them onto the heads of the mass of attackers below.

There were just too many Dervishes and the defenders were tired and hungry to the point of exhaustion. The great flood of dirty white robes, patched with coloured squares and rectangles, flowed over the walls and into the narrow streets and alleyways of Khartoum, their banners streaming behind them and death wherever they went. The fleeing civilians were butchered as they ran to hide and the soldiers of the garrison were cut down or shot as they retreated towards the more open spaces of the city centre. There, the last of the soldiers went down in blood and anguish and there, on the steps of his house, Gordon was speared and hacked to death and his head carried in triumph to the Mahdi.

A MARTYR OF EMPIRE

Woolwich Arsenal in outer London has long been an army base and a home for the Royal Artillery. There, on January 28, 1833, a Gunner officer's son was born. He was Charles George Gordon.

Like his father, young Gordon became a soldier; but unlike his father, he chose the Royal Engineers and in 1852 was commissioned into the Corps of Royal Sappers and Miners. Gordon had a good mind for mathematics and logic, one of three outstanding characteristics, the second of which was undoubted courage. At the seige of Sevastopol in the Crimean War, he displayed an almost reckless bravery which brought him to the attention of his superiors and led to his promotion to captain.

In 1860 Gordon volunteered to join the British forces fighting in the so-called Arrow War, a savage flare-up in China brought on by unequal trade treaties. He was one of the soldiers who marched into Peking, where he personally took charge of the burning of the Emperor's Summer Palace. For five years Gordon lived and worked in China — leading his Engineers in strengthening Shanghai's defences against rebels and becoming comander of the city's defence force, a 3,500-strong peasant army called "The Ever Victorious Force".

By the time he returned to England in 1865, he was known to press and public as "Chinese" Gordon, a nickname that would remain with him all through his life. His next years were spent in a quiet posting as commander of the Royal Engineers depot at Gravesend in the south of England. And it was in those rural precincts that his third major trait came to the fore — his adherence to a mystical, almost fanatical kind of Christianity.

In the spring of 1873, Gordon accepted an invitation from the Khedive of Egypt, who was fond of foreign appointees, to be a provincial governor in the Sudan, a post for which he was eminently well-qualified, it was thought, because of his engineering, military and foreign experience. And, indeed, he performed well. He mapped the Upper Nile, established a line of guard-posts and way-stations along the river southwards to what is now Uganda, put down rebellious tribes and suppressed the slave trade. The Khedive eventually appointed him Governor-General of the Sudan and he stayed until 1880 when ill-health forced him back to England.

Not that he rested for long. During the following three years he served in India, China again, Mauritius and South Africa. In 1884 it was back to Egypt again, having by this time assumed almost legendary status both in that country and in his own, where he was regarded by an adoring public as a hero of the Empire. His portrait at the time shows him as a broad-browed, handsome man, sombre and with a look of deep melancholy.

He left England in 1884 for the last time, reappointed Governor-General of the Sudan and with instructions from his own government to help evacuate Egyptian troops from the Sudan; in effect, abandoning it to Muslim rebels led by the Mahdi. Gordon reached Khartoum in February and, almost a year later, two days before his 52nd birthday, was killed by a rebel spearman.

General Charles George Gordon.

Broken lances symbolising glorious death, soldiers weep at the grave of the fallen hero.

Reactions were swift and fierce. In Britain, Queen Victoria, whose distaste for Gladstone and his attitudes and actions was well known, wrote a distraught letter to Gordon's sister, Augusta: "How shall I write to you or attempt to express what I feel! To think of your dear, noble, heroic brother, who served his country and his Queen so truly, so heroically, with a self sacrifice so edifying to the world, not having been rescued, is to me grief inexpressible! The stain left upon England!" An angry roar went up all over Britain for a punitive expedition.

In Australia, the Overland Telegraph that had been completed in 1872 brought the news of Gordon's death two weeks after it had occurred — almost as soon as it had reached London. And there was a resounding echo of the British Lion's roar of anger. Within hours, the acting Premier of New South Wales, William Bede Dalley, cabled London and offered the government and the War Office an expeditionary force to join whatever punitive strike might be made against the Mahdi. This immediate and practical offer was followed within days by similar ones from Victoria, Queensland, South Australia and New Zealand, but only the original offer was accepted. There was some doubt that the others could get to the scene of action in time.

There was no delay as far as the NSW contingent was concerned. Although the only military training in the colony till then had been for local service, although there was no organisational structure to handle the task, and although hardly a soul knew anything about likely conditions at the fighting front, within three weeks a force had been assembled, outfitted, equipped and was ready to go. The government had published, expressly for the NSW contingent's use, a handbook entitled *Suakin and the country of the Soudan*, which had been written by a Sydney doctor and explorer of Africa, Arthur Holroyd; and horses were bought, shipping space arranged for, ambulances found and fitted out, and piles of equipment, ammunition and supplies loaded into wagons ready for hold-stowage.

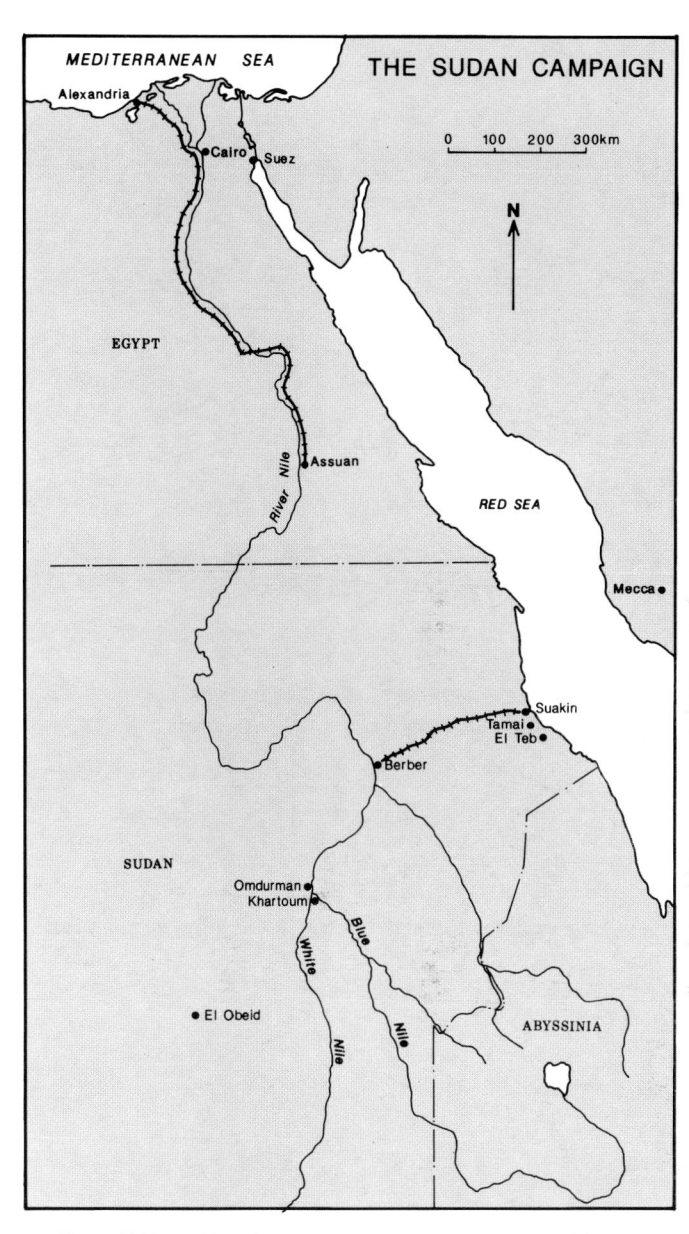

From 1883 to 1884, the Dervish army scored devastating blows against Anglo-Egyptian forces at El Obeid and El Teb. Then, General Gordon's murder at Khartoum precluded any diplomatic solutions, and Britain went to war in the Sudan. A NSW contingent landed at Suakin in March 1885, joined the British punitive expedition, and saw action in the Suakin hinterland, notably at Tamai wells.

As well, there were the volunteers, selected from among a mass of men, some of them ex-soldiers, many of them already trained to some level in local defence. There were 770 of them in the final count, led by their own 14-man band. Two batteries of Permanent Field Artillery were offered for service by NSW, but Britain accepted only one. It left behind its 16-pounder guns, which were considered too heavy for desert work; instead, six 9-pounder guns with ammunition and carriages were sent from England for the battery's use on arrival in the Sudan. There were also 500 men of the Infantry Battalion with two padres and an ambulance detachment of 35 officers and men bringing up the rear with supply wagons and extra horses.

Sydney's streets were thronged with cheering, singing crowds as the troops, brave in artillery blue-and-red and infantry scarlet-and-white, swung down to the two troopships, *Iberia* and *Australasian*, the band rattling and blaring out "The Girl I Left Behind Me". It was a splendid example of drive and initiative, fuelled by an ardour of patriotic feeling for the Mother Country, which few seemed inclined to doubt or mock. That the colonies had no interest in or connection with the events in the Sudan meant nothing; Britain was involved, and for many that was enough. On that Tuesday, March 3, 1885, when the troopships pulled away from Circular Quay, the *Sydney Mail* summed up the local feeling: "This is the day on which this Colony, not yet 100 years old, put forth its claims to be recognised as an integral portion of the British Empire, just as much as if it had been situated in the county of Middlesex instead of at the opposite end of the globe."

It was not that no voices were raised in protest. Sir Henry Parkes, politician, newspaper proprietor and self-proclaimed patriot, thunder-

A troopship lies anchored off the main Sudanese port of Suakin, the disembarkation point for the NSW contingent. The town was defended by a ring of forts and redoubts.

ed that Britain had no need of "our men" and that, more importantly, the colony had no constitutional powers to raise, pay for, or send off any such body of troops. That Parkes was correct was entirely beside the point on sailing day. The *Sydney Mail* pushed the popular message home hard: "Had it been necessary to raise double the number of troops, New South Wales could have provided them; and if the exigencies of the situation had required ten times that number all the Australian colonies would have raised them by united action!"

When the two ships pulled away through the harbour heads, they were carrying an unique body of men. The soliders of the past who had sailed that sea-road had been either soldiers of the Crown or mercenaries. The men who had volunteered to fight the Maoris in New Zealand had been uniformed and paid for their services, but had not been part of any unit in Australia. The Waikato Militia Regiments had been recruited in Victoria and NSW, shipped across the Tasman to New Zealand as berths were available, but not formed up into military units until they reached their destination. The Sudan contingent was the first formed body of Australian volunteer soldiers to go to fight overseas. They were, in truth, the first Australian expeditionary force.

Lord Loftus, Governor of NSW, addressed them as the anchor parties stood ready to weigh: "Soldiers of New South Wales, for the first time in the great history of the British Empire, a distant colony is sending, at her own cost, a completely equipped contingent of troops who have volunteered with enthusiasm of which only we who have witnessed it can judge."

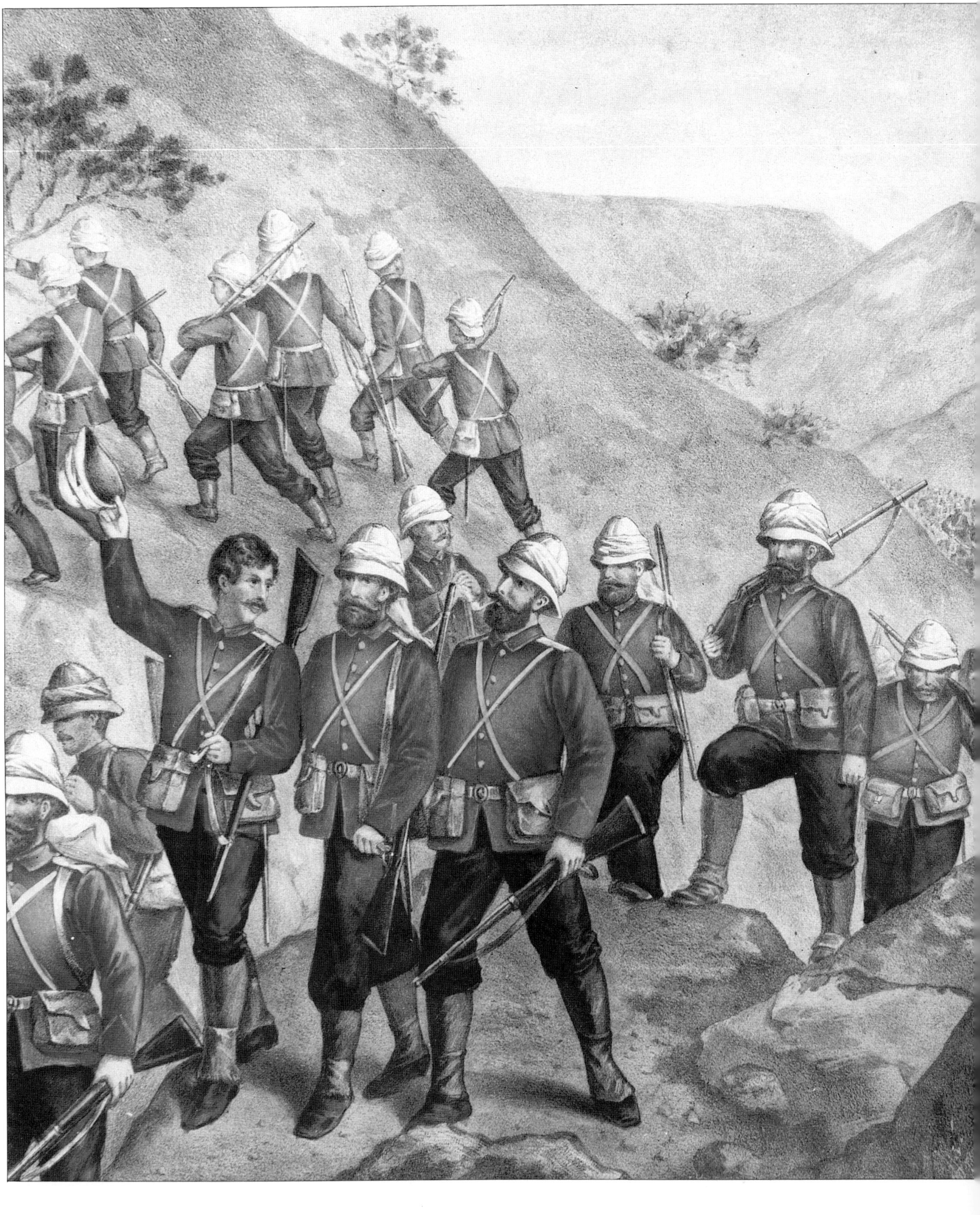

A small reconnoitring party splits from the main column as the NSW infantry and artillery battalions pass through a rocky ravine on their route march south to the Tamai Wells.

It was sad that so much passion and planning and patriotism should have gone into such a paltry affair.

High up on the right shoulder of Africa, the epaulette of the Red Sea giving it a stretch of coastline, sits the land that in the 19th century was usually spelled "Soudan", its people variously and belittlingly known as "Fuzzy-Wuzzies" or "Whirling Dervishes". Stretching massively down for a third of the continent's length, from Egypt to what was then Uganda and westward for 1,600 kilometres from Abyssinia (now known as Ethiopia), the land was a game-hunter's paradise in the swamp and rainforest of the south and central grasslands; in the north, where the desert held bleak sway, only the waters of the Nile gave relief. As well, it had always been the major supply route south from Egypt to Khartoum.

The main port on the African coast of the Red Sea from the 15th century to the 19th century was Suakin, and the British had long planned to build a railway from there west to Berber, to shorten the supply route towards Khartoum. Military operations around Suakin had been instigated to clear the area so construction of the railway could go ahead unimpeded. It was to the low jetties of the tortuous harbour of Suakin that the Australian troopships tied up on March 29, 1885. The Australian contingent marched ashore to begin an association with Africa-at-arms which would last through four wars.

The soldiers already in the Sudan when the Australians arrived were all too familiar with the harsh conditions there. They were men of the punitive expedition that had arrived too late to save Gordon: Indians of the 15th Sikh Regiment and the Bengal Cavalry. There were Royal Marines and troops of the Royal Horse Artillery and the three Regiments of the Foot Guards — Coldstream, Grenadier and Scots. For those three Household regiments, as for the Berkshire Regiment, the Sudanese battle honour was somewhere in the middle of a long, long list commemorating victories on scores of battlefields around the world. The Coldstream and the Grenadiers, for example, began their tally of honours with "Tangier — 1690".

For the Australian Army, the first battle honour to be won was "Suakin — 1885". They earned the honour under Major-General Sir Gerald Graham, who placed them among the elite, brigading them with the legendary Guards. They became less sure that it was an honour when they found that their first task was a 65-kilometre march inland under a pitiless sun. They were heading for the large village of Tamai which, because of its permanent deep wells, was a base for Osman Digna's guerrillas. For 16 hours the Australians and the Guards struggled across the broiler of the coastal plain, marching for 55 minutes, stopping for five; not being allowed to sit or stand still lest the muscles set, and sipping luke-warm water from their canteens only when permission was given.

With them marched the correspondent of the *Sydney Morning Herald*, W. J. Lambie, and he drew a clear picture of British military methods which had changed little in fact from the days of the Crimea: "The force detailed for the advance on Tamai was formed up at about half-past seven on three sides of a square with a strong column in the centre. The Berkshire Regiment was in front, the 15th Sikhs on the left face, the Marines on the right face and the Guards Brigade, including the Australians, was formed in column of companies in the centre; the Royal Horse Artillery on the right, the Bengal Cavalry on the flanks and the Mounted Infantry in front. Inside the square were two 7-pounder mountain screw-guns on mules, two 7-pounders on wheels and three 9-pounder rocket tubes."

Considering that the enemy, though great in numbers, was armed with some captured rifles but mainly with old muskets and *jezails*, their home-made, brass-bound long guns, and family swords and spears, the solidly formal British advance and its weight of arms seems to have been a good example of overkill.

The Australians were sent, sweating and stumbling under the lash of the sun, from their position in the centre of the advance up to extend the right wing, facing into a ravine. No sooner had they formed up than their No. 1 Company was pushed forward and into action. They moved up under harassing fire from enemy positions, the Sudanese firing inaccurately but quite heavily; three of the Australians were hit, Private Walter Harrison in the shoulder, Private Charles Downey in the foot and Private William Learoyd of the Ambulance Corps took a furrowing graze in the scalp. No doubt the wounds were painful, but it is difficult to find much drama in them, even though these three men were half the total casualties in the British force that day.

When the screw-guns opened up and sent their shells neatly into the enemy positions, small-arms fire from the ravine and the rocks quickly died away. The infantry pushed forward, sergeants and warrant-officers yelling at their men to keep their lines steady and "dress properly by the centre", an almost impossible task as they slipped and scrambled across the ravine. The Indian Lancers and the Mounted Infantry swung wide around the infantry and into the village ahead of them, where they methodically put the tinder-dry thatched huts to the torch. By the time the foot soldiers moved through the smoke, their tunics black with sweat, no enemy was to be seen. The Tamai wells had been captured.

It hardly had the ring of high romance about it and seemingly little of the stinging spice of danger, but it was as close as the Australians were to get to any sort of proper action in that odd little campaign. By the middle of that year, 1885, the Mahdi was dead and in the years from then till close to the century's end, British arms were actively engaged in the Sudan, culminating in the great charge of cavalry at Omdurman in 1898 in which the young Winston Churchill took part.

The Australian volunteers, all well-equipped and uniformed, well-armed and horsed, were used in less immediately military ways. They became skilled at building "zarebas", camp enclosures made of heavily-spiked thorn bushes; Major-General A. J. Lyon-Fremantle,

Osman Digna's Dervish army beats back a British advance at Tamai Wells on March 13, 1884. Licking their wounds, the British retreated to Egypt and the unsubdued Dervishes besieged Berber and Khartoum.

THE DERVISH DOWNFALL

The Arabs of the Sudan were never able to match the modern army Britain and its empire could pit against them. Relying, in battle, on implicit faith in the will of God, the Arabs would charge into organised rifle and cannon fire without flinching. Their weapons were primitive, even by the standards of the end of the 19th century; captured hand and long guns were the best of them, but these fierce warriors, were deadly fighters with long, slightly curved swords or heavy-bladed spears.

The Dervishes were among the toughest groups in the family of Muslim nations, and they were considered to be very close to Allah. They were nomads; wanderers leading lives of self-denial, practising unusual forms of devotion such as wearing only the roughest of clothing, keeping extremely long fasts, and probably the best known to Westerners, whirling and dancing to reed pipe music. It was from this last ritual that the common name of Whirling Dervish came, but to British and Australian soldiers they were known as Fuzzy-Wuzzies, their reckless bravery earning them considerable respect.

The Dervish leader, the Mahdi, died at Omdurman on June 22, 1885; some reports claim smallpox or typhoid was the cause, while others say he was poisoned. He was succeeded by the Kalifa Abdullah, who took control of the whole of the Sudan, and under his watch it remained a restless land for the next decade. During that time France and Italy showed increasing colonial interest in the Nile Valley and the British Government decided to reoccupy the Sudan.

The man to do it was Major-General Sir Horatio Kitchener, Sirdar of the Egyptian Army. He moved methodically up the line of the Nile, his British and Egyptian troops supported by a flotilla of river gunboats, his engineers building a railway as he marched, ensuring his logistical support as he moved towards a confrontation with Britain's old enemies, Osman Digna and Abdullah. The remorseless advance met and defeated fanatical opposition in a series of battles in what turned out to be a long, slow war. The first engagement was at Dongola in September 1896; the last was not until two years later when on September 2, 1898, the Battle of Omdurman was fought.

Kitchener's army of 26,000 — half British, half well-trained Egyptians — was attacked six kilometres out of Omdurman, Abdullah sweeping on them with 40,000 wild and brave tribesmen. But Kitchener's artillery included 20 weapons still new on the battlefield — machine-guns. The Sudanese fell in great swathes, then Kitchener ordered a counter-attack, pushing his troops towards Omdurman. In a full-blooded cavalry charge, the 21st Lancers rode over Abdullah's men and broke them completely.

Omdurman ended the war. The Sudanese casualties were more than 10,000 dead, a similar number wounded and 5,000 taken prisoner. Kitchener lost 500 all told and become Earl Kitchener of Khartoum and of Broome, the darling of the Empire.

Private W.E. Learoyd of the Ambulance Corps was wounded in the brief battle at Tamai, April 3, 1885. His discharge papers cite his Egypt medal and Khedive Star for Sudan.

commanding the Guards Brigade, commended them on their camp buildings and on their ingenuity in improvising means of shelter.

Most of their duties came under the general heading of "railway fatigues", unglamorous but essential work to ensure the single-line track was kept clear of Mahdist forces. With armed sentries posted to watch over neatly piled rifles, the Australians shovelled and levelled ballast, re-spiked loose sleeper-ties and cleared sword-sharp and sun-dried grass and weeds from alongside the rails. Others were detailed to patrol stretches of the line, monotonous and wearying work with no enemy in sight even though an occasional bullet came out of the seemingly empty countryside and passed harmlessly into the rocks beyond. At least such random and infrequent fire gave the Australians the excuse for loosing off a few rounds in return. There seemed to be no casualties on either side from the exchanges.

These labouring and patrolling tasks were duties which were neither dangerous nor exciting, and that probably explains why there was no difficulty in finding 50 volunteers willing to be detached to serve with the Camel Corps, a scouting formation raised with Egyptian funds but with British officers and a mix of colonial volunteers. Several of them volunteered to stay on with that corps, but the offer was rejected as was the NSW Government's offer to Britain to have the contingent go on to serve in the Mediterranean or India, where a crisis in Anglo-Russian relations had developed over an incident at a village on the Afghanistan border. The Australians, however, were to go home, and that proved the most dangerous part of the whole expedition.

The first Australian soldier to die on active overseas service was Private Robert Weir of the 4th Infantry Company of the Sudan contingent. He died of dysenteric fever on board the hospital ship *Ganges* as it was tied up at the Suakin docks. Two others died also, from typhoid illness, at Suakin: Gunner Edward Lewis from the artillery battery and Private P. Jackson of the infantry batallion. Three more, Private John Col-

The NSW contingent received a gloomy homecoming. One veteran recalled later: "Our return did not appear popular and I gathered that too many of us had come back."

lister, and Gunners Thomas Coburn and James Robertson, died of fever at Colombo, Ceylon, on the way home aboard the troopship *Arab*, and then from Colombo to Albany in Western Australia, one in every 10 men turned up on average to the daily sick parade; the veterinary surgeon, Captain Anthony Willows, died and was buried at sea. In a bitter last blow, two men died immediately following the contingent's return to Sydney; Private Richard Perry while the troops were in quarantine at Sydney's North Head, and Private Martin Guest as a result of a cold caught in the drenching rain that dampened the contingent's welcome-home celebrations.

There had been no deaths in battle and the whole brief affair was, perhaps, best summed up by Colonel A. J. Bennett, a member of the contingent. He wrote: "Intense heat, dust, insects, thirst and stench from bodies of dead Arabs and animals provided sufficient horrors of war, with dysentery and sunstroke claiming tremendous toll. A few skirmishes and many weary marches provided much sweat but little glory."

The glory was yet to come. And the death.

SUDAN EXPEDITION

Huge crowds jostle at Sydney's docks for the best view of the white-helmeted NSW contingent embarking for the Sudan, March 3, 1885.

"We were soldiers, and Sydney shouted it from the housetops."

BEATING THE DRUM

The hastily formed force of 734 men of the New South Wales contingent for the Sudan were given a clamorous Sydney farewell on March 3, 1885. Despite offers of troops from other Australian colonies that went unheeded, public excitement over the Sudan campaign led it to be popularly called "the great adventure".

The troops, however, were in the Sudan for only seven weeks and saw little action. The six who died did so on their return voyage. But the Sudan affair set a precedent for Australia's military involvement with Britain in future overseas wars, giving Australia's first expeditionary force of regular troops a taste of Africa; it would be the first of four campaigns in which Australians, many of whom came from outback regions, would find themselves in a war, often fought in desert conditions, on that continent.

Above: Volunteers for the NSW Infantry Battalion wait to be issued uniforms on the parade ground at Victoria Barracks. Right: In a mixture of uniforms from their respective NSW regiments, regulars bound for the Sudan appear jaunty on the morning of their departure. Unlike civilian volunteers, they had some military training.

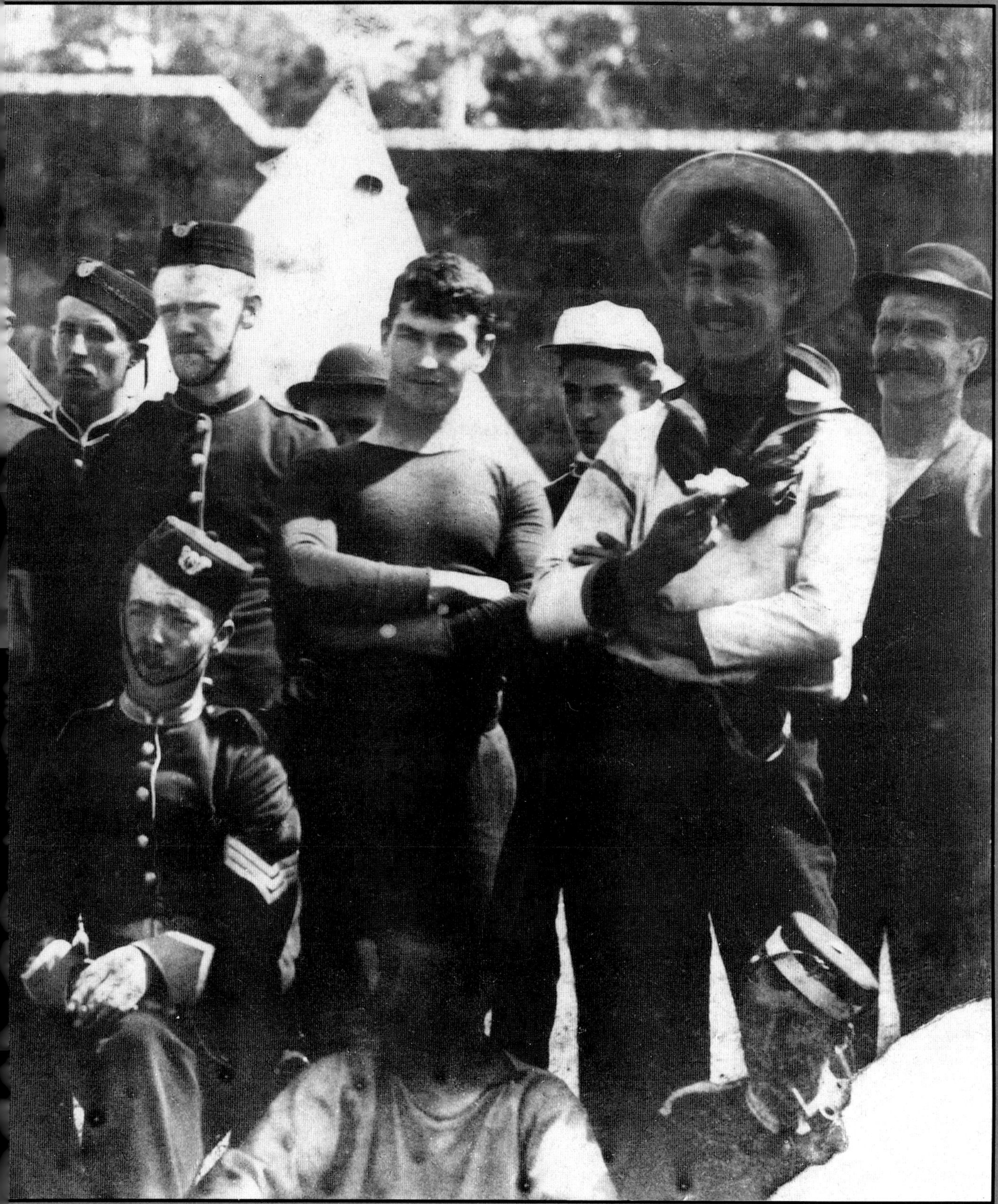

The British Camel corps, the Desert Hussars, camp near Handub. The Corps included 50 NSW volunteers, though all Australian infantry could ride camels.

Wearing "mushroom" sun helmets, the NSW artillery battalion guard a 9-pounder cannon.

Private Robert Weir's mates pay homage at his desolate grave in Suakin. Weir died on a hospital ship tied up at the port.

3

A SAILOR'S CAMPAIGN

China surged toward outright war as fanatical "Boxer" rebels took control. Australia proudly sent a naval brigade to join an international peace-keeping force there, but was the junior partner in another British triumph.

The French called the period leading up to the 20th century "La Belle Epoque", the lovely time. Then, as the midnight chimes rang 1899 away, they said it was "La Fin du Siècle", the end of an era. However dubious that first claim may have been, the second was undoubtedly right; the advent of the new century marked the end of much that was traditional and accepted as permanent. A young English physicist called Ernest Rutherford had just published a paper about mysterious things called alpha and beta particles and the prospects of further atomic exploration. An earnest group of internationalists was putting together the first peace conference at The Hague. And Britain — more or less as usual — was at war.

Britain was accustomed to being in that position. It had a very professional army, well used to battlefields of all kinds, all sizes, and in all temperatures. Because of the places and people within the territories of the British Empire, any of its long-service soldiers who had seen overseas action was likely to think of an enemy in terms of "a native", African of one sort or another but always black, Burmese, Indian, Chinese, or any one of a dozen "savages". It was an attitude which was

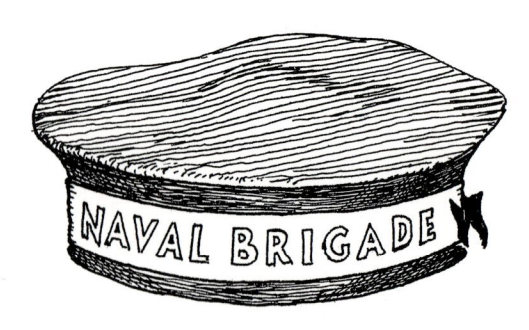

Cloth over leather cap which replaced the old straw panama-style hat. The "tally" (ribbon) bore the brigade name.

common down the ranks from general to private, the British army being a stolid body of men, bone-deep in bigotry and largely unchanging. Yet, it was a well disciplined and a very able force, capable of fighting more than one small war at a time.

In the colonies of Australia, the local and independent defence forces were a different matter altogether. They had grown into sizeable bodies, regular and volunteer, and among those volunteers were many outside the cities, men accustomed to the use and care of horses and to living rough. Britain, however, was still seen as the shield and buckler, and the colonies ranked low as an army-producing base. Local defence forces were not well-funded, and many of the volunteer units provided their own uniforms, mounts, equipment and even, in some cases, weapons and ammunition.

And yet, in 1899 and 1900, the colonies offered themselves in support of British arms and objectives in two simultaneous wars on two distant continents. Australia dispatched a force to South Africa which would eventually stay there long past the colonies' federation into a Commonwealth of states, but little more than six months after Australia put together that first contingent to the Boer War, it was organising another expeditionary force to sail in a quite different direction.

At the turn of the century, China had become an exotic and dangerous beast. Huge, and ancient, and sprawling, it offered tantalising glimpses of great riches and wondrous treasures. Aside from the fragile beauty of exquisite porcelain, of the fiercely graceful dogs and dragons cast in bronze, and the delicacy of painted screen and scrolls and lengths of gossamer silk, there were the more prosaic, and equally valuable, herbs and spices, exotic roots and plants and fragrant teas. Together with the ever-present rumours of gold and jewels in the unknown land, these trade goods brought merchantmen from America and Russia, from Germany and Portugal and France and, predominantly, from Britain.

The old land of Cathay, Kublai Khan's Xanadu was still there, shining and golden, but it had been tormented by Western greed for new territory. Its skin had been pierced by the barbs and arrows of European trade; the venom on their tips was smuggled opium which gradually took the place of the currency that Westerners paid for the goods they coveted. The balance of trade eventually swung entirely in favour of the West with large amounts of silver, as well as trade goods, going to pay for the opium. The whole assault of the West's armed commercialism was sweetened — or, at least, concealed — by the thrust of Christianity. To traditional and conservative Chinese just about everything the Europeans did was wrong; they showed no respect for family, they were gross, clumsy, and destructive. They made no attempt to trade with grace, only to buy with crudity and, worst of all, their missionaries were seducing people away from the gongs and dragons of proper worship.

As the 1890s wore away, as the "foreign devils" bit more and more deeply into Chinese territory and customs, secret societies that were violently anti-European began to form. But, when Europe's ambassadors sought protection for their nationals in China, the lacquered and bejewelled Dowager Empress Tzu Hsi held out diplomatically helpless hands, her interpreters presenting the contradiction that the all-powerful Manchu Empress was, strangely, unable to influence the fanatics. She conceded, however, that something should be done to curb them, especially the most violent, and most popular group, *I-ho-ch'uan*, which was daily growing angrier and stronger. Its name translated roughly as the "Society of Righteous and Harmonious Fists", and they soon became known to Western correspondents as "the Boxers".

Throughout 1899 the more militant Chinese societies combined in a campaign of terror against all Westerners and converted Chinese Christians. Many of the Empress' militia helped the insurgents and there were scores of violent outbreaks. Missionaries and other civilians were murdered, rape and pillage were

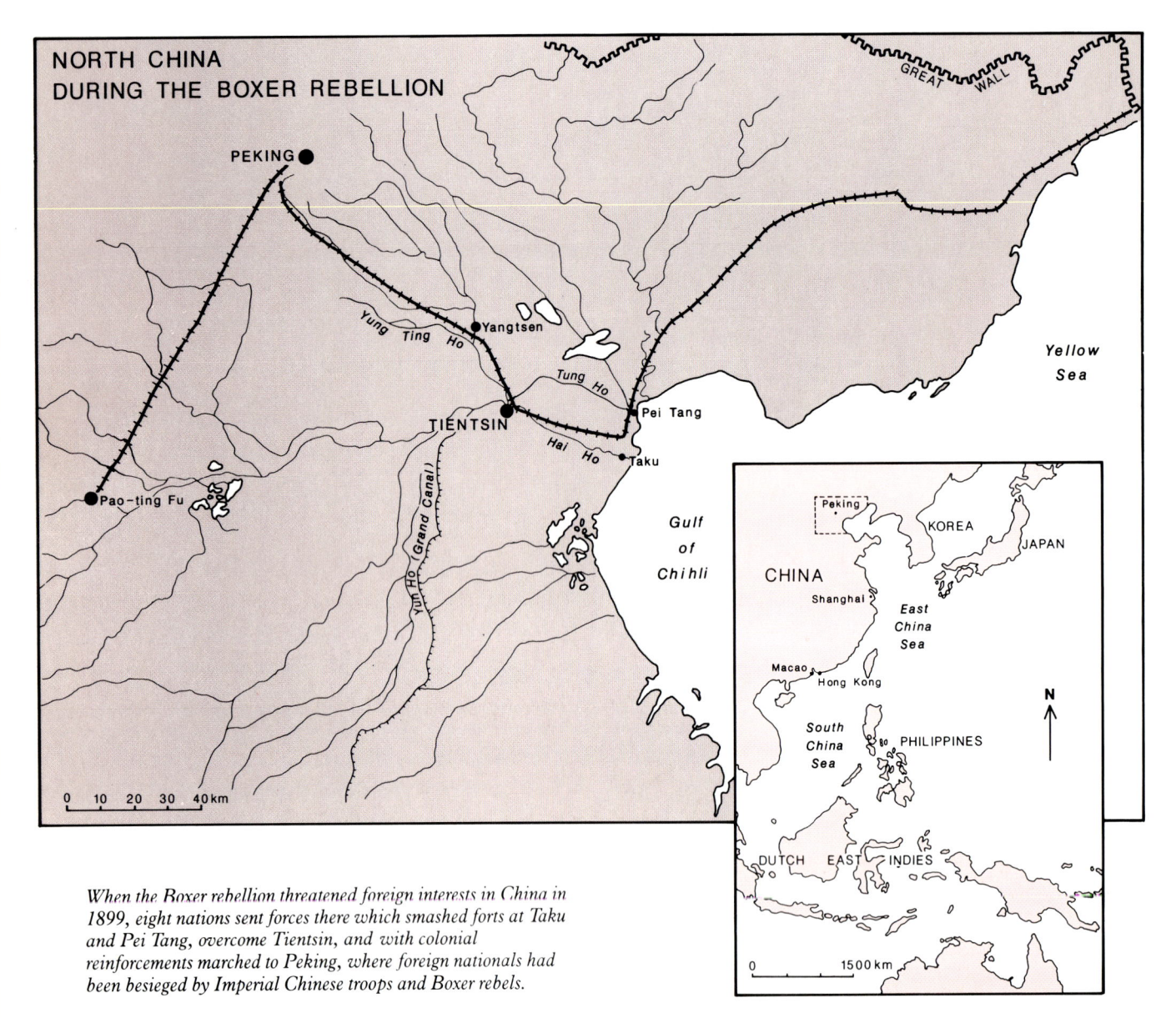

When the Boxer rebellion threatened foreign interests in China in 1899, eight nations sent forces there which smashed forts at Taku and Pei Tang, overcome Tientsin, and with colonial reinforcements marched to Peking, where foreign nationals had been besieged by Imperial Chinese troops and Boxer rebels.

common, and the destruction of European-owned property was widespread across the north of China. It was plain to see that the statements issued from Peking by the Empress, while expressing pious hopes for peace, now almost openly supported the Boxers. In the last of the North China winter — a season bleak enough of its own accord — there was a near general uprising and, by March 1900, the Western nations were forced into action, ostensibly to protect their nationals in China. The underlying reason was, of course, to protect their territorial and trade ambitions.

Warships from Britain, Italy and the United States anchored menacingly off the coast near Taku, the nearest port to Peking. France, Germany, Austria and Russia, as well as Japan, had armed contingents of varying strengths on the way. But by the end of May the situation at Peking had deteriorated, causing members of the city's diplomatic corps to ask urgently for reinforcements of legation guards engaged in protecting Western refugees who had fled there to escape the growing Boxer terror. In reply almost 500 soldiers, sailors and marines from eight nations were sent by train into Peking to take up guard duties.

Under the command of Vice Admiral Sir Edward Seymour, a further force of 2,000 marines and sailors, 900 of them British, were put ashore and left by train for Peking on June 10. They were well equipped for a field campaign with a number of machine-guns and a troop of seven field-guns, although there was no feeling that the Boxer insurgents were strong enough to face them. However, the Dowager Empress chose this moment to show her true colours openly, and sent Imperial troops to join the Boxers in such great strength that the invaders were forced to retreat to the city of Tientsin, where they were then besieged. After hearing of Seymour's plight, Rear Admiral J.A.T. Bruce, second-in-command of the British fleet still at anchor, put another small relieving force ashore, but when even further cries for reinforcements were received he had no more troops available.

As the foreign force waited for support, the Chinese secured the four heavily-gunned forts at Taku that guarded the entrance to the Hai Ho River, the best inland route to Tientsin, which, up river from there, was known as the Pei Ho. But on June 17, 1900, the forts were stormed, and four Chinese Navy destroyers based just inshore were captured. The way was now safe for the landing of the foreign reinforcements. The war with China had formally begun.

By that time another war of Britain's was well under way in South Africa — and there were Australians already fighting there. Men in training who had been thinking of the flat heat of the veldt now began to wonder whether they were more likely to be of use in the Far East. But they were soldiers and this was to be largely a sailor's campaign.

By August 1900 there would be eight nations with ships in Chinese waters and troops on Chinese land and, though the terms "United Nations" and "multi-national" had not then been coined, either would have suited the forces opposed by the Society of the Righteous

A European missionary catches a wheelbarrow "taxi". Missionaries were the main target of the Boxer's anti-foreign sentiments.

A fresh-faced lieutenant, H. E. Lofts, commanded the NSW Marine Light Infantry.

and Harmonious Fists. In that August another country's name was added to the roll; Australia was, again for Britain's sake, sending a contingent to China.

Not that it was as purely national as that. Each colony had its own forces and, in fact, it was South Australia which was the first to offer aid, with New South Wales and Victoria hard behind. The South Australians put forward what amounted to their entire navy — Her Majesty's Colonial Ship, the cruiser *Protector*, a small but heavily armed, steel-hulled cruiser — and, after some debate, the British Government accepted the offer, as long as the ship came under Royal Navy command.

The *Protector* was one of a number of vessels belonging to the colonial governments used purely for local defence. The Australian colonies were also partners in the establishment of the Auxiliary Squadron, a formation of warships designed to protect sea-trade in Australasian waters, in addition to the Royal Navy's own Imperial Squadron based in Australia. The fleet was paid for, in part, by the colonies and New Zealand, and it was an indication of the growing strength, importance and self-confidence of the colonies that they were able to impose a specific stipulation on the Admiralty in return for that payment; none of the warships could be sailed from the Australian Station without the consent of the colonial governments.

The request for that consent had been made on June 28 and it was agreed to at once. Further, Sir William Lyne, then Premier of NSW, sweetened the agreement by adding the offer of a naval brigade which had been readying itself to go to South Africa. The War Office in London snapped up the offer without hesitation, and when Victoria immediately offered a second brigade, the War Office quickly accepted that one as well.

Australia's regular army organisations were not going to be much help in this campaign as the war against the Boers in South Africa was drawing away most of the colony's volunteer-soldiers; by mid-1900 four contingents of troops had gone. The colonial navies, on the other hand, provided an immediately available pool of trained men, the crews being professional seamen, engaged full-time. Around this core in each colony were the reservist-volunteers, many of them ex-naval men from all branches — deck, guns and engines. These reservists were mustered into naval brigades in which the training was geared towards coastal defence by sailors capable of ship-handling, as well as performing as soldiers under arms.

In the late afternoon on July 30, 1900, the transport ship *Salamis*, chartered for the purpose by Her Majesty's Government, left Melbourne for Sydney. She carried the 200 Victorian Naval Brigade Volunteers originally destined for South Africa who, a few days later, were joined by 260 more from NSW. With that second half of the contingent was a small group of men looking conspicuously different in khaki among the mass of navy-blue.

They had come from Victoria Barracks in Sydney, where men had been waiting to be placed into units planned for the South African campaign. Word had been passed that there were vacancies for any who wished to volunteer for China, especially men with seafaring experience. There were a number of volunteers, but they said they were soldiers and would not go as sailors. The bluejackets of the naval

Above: The baked mud ramparts and stake barricades of the forts at Taku were no obstacle to British and French forces on an earlier march to sack Peking in 1860. Below: Similar scenes of carnage inside the forts followed the multinational assault on these strongholds on June 17, 1900, which succumbed easily, allowing the force to land and begin quelling the uprising.

brigade, in their turn, said that they would not allow the soldiers into their ranks. A fine compromise was reached when 25 men were selected and formed into a brand-new unit called the NSW Marine Light Infantry under the command of H.E. Lofts, a young lieutenant of the 1st Australian Infantry.

On August 6, as the Sydney contingent was finalising its fitting-out and completing an exhausting round of formal farewells, HMCS *Protector* sailed from Adelaide bound for Sydney to load ammunition and rifles before following *Salamis* to China via Hong Kong. *Salamis* sailed on August 8, with its own ship handlers, rifle-and-cutlass-carrying soldiers, Marines, ambulance detachment and band. The men were being paid 7s 6d a day while away from Australia, 1s 6d in the hand and 6s to the families left behind.

The NSW sailors and the Marines were armed with early Lee-Metford magazine rifles and with bayonets which the Royal Naval establishment in Sydney had passed on to them. The Victorians carried older Martini-Enfield rifles with triangular bayonets, the rifle-barrels specially adapted from a .577 calibre to take the same .303 ammunition as their NSW partners used. In the hold of the *Salamis* were the contingent's field-guns and transport—ancient five-barrelled Nordenfeldt hand-levered machine-guns, cumbrous muzzle-loading 9-pounder cannon, and utility carts sensibly brought by the Victorians.

After 18 days at sea, *Salamis* dropped anchor in the harbour at Hong Kong. There the Royal

The troop ship S.S. Salamis leaves Sydney Harbour on August 8, 1900, carrying the Victorian and NSW contingents to war.

Navy's quartermasters took one look at the age and miscellany of weapons the contingent had brought with them and swiftly organised a change-over. The troops were all given new-model Lee-Metfords, and .45-calibre Maxim machine-guns were issued, equipped with both deck mountings and wheels. The men from Australia were also given the best of the available field-guns, 12-pounder breech-loaders.

The contingent had now been re-equipped, standardised, drilled for display, inspected, and declared satisfactory. The senior naval officer, Captain A.C. Clarke RN, said in his dispatch: "I have never seen a finer body of men, they are clean and smart looking. Our country is fortunate in having so many staid and disciplined men willing to volunteer for active service. I understand that many more may be had if required."

His last sentence made it sound as though the men were little more than a commodity, and certainly the captain was doing no more than echoing a general British sentiment when he addressed the men.

"Remember you are doing good work for Queen and country," he said. "They call you the Australian Contingent, a very good name, but remember this — we all regard you as the British Contingent from Australia."

Far from causing offence, the captain's words brought a cheer from the men. But, there was no cheering when they reached their station in China. No one was expecting them. The Royal Navy, the world's most powerful, lacked any

NSW Naval Brigade men with their antique 9-pounder cannon. The force's guns were updated by the British in Hong Kong.

sort of telegraphic equipment. (The German warships, however, did have Signor Marconi's invaluable instrument.) On arrival the ship remained unknown till flag signals flew and *Salamis* steamed in to join the great mass of warships and transports anchored 19 kilometres off the North China coast where the water was still deep enough to take their hulls. There were 150 of them, the number staying fairly constant as daily sailings were balanced by fresh ships carrying more troops.

The first reports of the war the men of *Salamis* received were that Tientsin's walls had been stormed and the city taken by an expeditionary force, which, with further reinforcements, had gone on to Peking and met with similar success in relieving that city on August 14. Then came the bad news. Shore-side accommodation was at a premium, and the contingent in *Salamis* could not stay aboard for more than two days because the ship was ordered to sail out with a detachment of Royal Marines returning to Hong Kong. The Royal Navy's quick answer to that problem was to split the Australians.

The Victorians were ordered to establish themselves in one of the Taku forts and the New South Welshmen were to be sent off to Peking. The grumbling had hardly begun when the orders were amended: the Australian Naval Brigade of the China Field Force was to be quartered in and would operate from Tientsin.

It was believed that the Boxers were still thick and fierce around Tientsin. The Australians offloaded their machine-guns and their four 12-pounders into the barges which were to take them from their anchorage 25 kilometres into the shallows of the Hai Ho River. They wrote letters home, cleaned their rifles yet again, put keen edges on their bayonets, looked into their ammunition pouches and prepared for action. If not quite at the front, they were certainly heading in the right direction.

They passed through a landscape strange in more than the simple physical sense. The country was well-watered, even swampy, and grew rice, millet and some wheat — or would have done if the paddies and higher fields were not thick with weeds. Peasant families had fled by the thousand in the face of actual or even threatened fighting and to the newly arrived Australians it must have seemed that the population of this arc of China was a mixture of Europeans, Indians and Japanese, and all of them soldiers.

The railway which had been built from the coast of Tientsin and beyond was a narrow-gauge line which had been broken by the Boxers, repaired by coolie labour working for the Royal Navy, then taken over by the Russian contingent who worked it on a catch-as-catch-can basis. The waterways included a man-made stretch of "Grand Canal", a system of cuttings that acted as a link between the waterways and could be plied by small junks, poled punts, and dory-type boats and rafts. It was reliable enough to take the Naval Brigade safely to the dockside at Tientsin where they were taken under the wing of Britain's contingent from the Indian Army — a Sikh band to march them to the camp which they were to share with the Bengal Lancers, a Punjabi infantry regiment and the Madras Pioneers. A day spent settling in, buying some stocks of local food and, inevitably, parading for inspection, was at once followed by marching orders. They were to provide 300 men to join a force to capture the Chinese-occupied forts at Pei Tang, a coastal town whose fortifications menaced the railway line as it headed inland.

There was a solid enough force going into the field: 8,000 all told from Russia, Germany, Austria, British India and even the Chinese troops of the newly formed Wei-hai-wei Regiment with their British officers. The Australian contingent, 150 each from Victoria and NSW, were elated at the thought of seeing some action; what they saw was somewhere between farce and folly.

With no experience in land-campaigning they took the command to "travel light" far too literally and left themselves short of a number of minor things and one major one — rations. They moved out of camp quickly and eagerly to board a train which they had been told

RIGHTEOUS AND HARMONIOUS FISTS

A Boxer chief and his "tribe" wield traditional Chinese weapons, scimitar-shaped pikes and broad three-pronged forks.

The Boxer movement was modelled on the many secret societies that have sprung up in China since ancient times to periodically challenge the authority of the Imperial Government. Though flood and famine caused great misery and discontent in rural China in the 1890s, the Boxers did not seek the downfall of the government of the day.

The Boxers had formed in direct response to the incursion of foreign powers in China and defied Imperial authority only in attacking foreigners protected by government-signed treaties. Main targets included hated Christian missionaries who, with Western business and government representatives, were called "primary devils", followed by Chinese Christian converts, known as "secondary devils".

The Boxer ethos was a strange mixture of Buddhist, Taoist and Confucian beliefs, and ideas drawn from popular plays and novels which extolled a traditional China free from foreign influence. The English-language newspaper the *North China Daily News* labelled them Boxers probably because they practised either Tai Chi meditational movements or martial-arts styled Chinese boxing, but the term could also have come from the translation of their Chinese name, I-Ho-Chu'an (Righteous and Harmonious Fists).

The Boxers were identified by their red shirts and a variety of red belts, sashes, turbans and armbands. Most recruits were either illiterate peasants or unemployed ex-soldiers, and membership of the society was restricted to men. In the spirit of traditionalism, the Boxers carried only medieval weapons when they charged into enemy gunfire chanting "Sha! Sha!" (Kill! Kill!). They believed, however, that they were invulnerable in combat, claiming that the Boxer killed in battle had been lax in his devotions or had transgressed against the laws of the society.

In 1897, two German missionaries were murdered and a wave of arson and murder swept across northern China, spread allegedly by the Boxers. Despite angry protests by foreign officials, provincial Chinese authorities in Shantung and Chihli were reluctant to engage the rebels, offering them tacit support instead. Chinese authorities in Peking, most notably Empress Tzu Hsi, also sympathised with the Boxers, and by June 1900, with an Imperial army in the city and bands of Boxers roaming the streets, the battlelines were drawn. Events then soon escalated to outright war between China and the foreign nations targeted by the Boxers from the start of the uprising.

Boxer prisoners of war suffer the humiliation of wearing cangues, portable pillories, usually reserved for common criminals.

A Japanese officer cleans his sword after the ritual decapitation of Boxer spies. European troops preferred firing parties to this Samurai method.

Boxers lunge at the "enemy", in a fearsome display of strength. Undaunted by hailing bullets, Boxers surged forward chanting "Kill! Kill!"

would move them up to a position close to the forts. Unfortunately, the Russians who were controlling the railway had made some sort of arrangement with the Germans and given them exclusive rail-travel rights. The Australians had to march back into Tientsin and wait at the dock for lighters to be loaded with mules, baggage, Indian troops and, at last, themselves.

By the time the tow down-river began it was full night and pouring rain; there seemed to be a sort of inevitability about the fact that, in total blackness and covered by sheets of water, the lighters grounded on a mudbank. Not to be put off, the men squelched and floundered ashore and, soaked and weary, headed towards their rendezvous with the main force. Eighteen hours later, out of condition and exhausted, foodless since the previous day except for a tinned meat and biscuit ration, they came to the battle line in the Russian sector to find to their disappointment and openly expressed rage that the battle was over.

Not that there had been a lot to it. The Chinese defenders had managed to slip out under cover of the rain-sodden darkness leaving only one gun and its men as a suicide rearguard. When the Russians stormed into the forts they found only half-a-dozen dead Chinese.

The next foray was to be against the Boxer fortress at Pao-ting Fu, where it was thought the Chinese government had gone when Peking was taken and the seige of the embassies lifted. Again there was to be an international force and again, almost at the last minute, the Australian contingent was split, the New South Welshmen to head for Peking and the Victorians to go to Pao-ting Fu.

The Victorians joined the column as it marched out of Tientsin on October 12, 1900; there were 7,500 men, horse, foot and guns and another 1,000 in the baggage-train. It was a 10-day march in which rations ran low, local livestock was killed for food, looting was common though poorly rewarded, and again, anti-climax was the end result. Pao-ting Fu had meekly surrendered and the closest the Australians came to the enemy was when they were sent to guard prisoners found guilty of murder. These were shot out-of-hand by a German firing-party, unlike the convicted city officials who were ritually beheaded by Japanese army swordsmen in a dramatic and very public way.

Pao-ting Fu having been suitably subdued, the international column began the march back to Tientsin, concentrating on driving home the lesson of subjugation. They left a trail of devastated villages and dead Chinese behind them, looting where they could, burning and shooting at will. On the march up the Australians had commandeered a number of mules from a small village; on the return march six of the peasants who owned the animals tried to take them back. They were caught and, a half-hour later, having been convicted of stealing their own mules, they were shot. After 25 days in the field, the Victorians arrived back in Tientsin having traipsed more than 300 kilometres without seeing the enemy, let alone coming under his fire. Instead, executions and arson, and plundering and ransacking were their means to the spoils of war.

While the Victorians had been part of the useless and murderous rampage to Pao-ting Fu, the New South Welshmen were taking on what amounted to civic, almost domestic duties in Peking. They had arrived in the city, parts of which were still battered from its torturous 55-day seige, on October 22. It had been a 160-kilometre march to get there, a 12-day trudge broken and cheered by a stopover in Yangtsen, a town garrisoned by a United States Marine regiment. It was surely the first time troops from Australia found, as their descendents were to find in many other places, that U.S. military detachments never stint if it can be avoided. The Australians were able to supplement their standard and dull rations with tinned fruits, bacon, tobacco, tinned salmon and coffee and all at cheap-rate canteen prices.

They were escorted into Peking a week after that cheerful encounter, a Sikh bugle band ahead of them, a Baluchi pipe-band behind

THE SIEGE OF PEKING

Foreigners based in Peking found their situation deteriorating rapidly from May 1900, when the Empress Dowager, Tzu Hsi, allowed Boxers to stage anti-foreigner demonstrations within the walled city. Then, in early June, matters worsened; an 18,000-strong Imperial Chinese army arrived to reinforce the thousands of undisciplined Boxers already swarming the streets. On June 19, the foreign diplomatic corps received an ultimatum ordering them to leave Peking, but before they could act the head of the German legation, Baron von Kettler, was murdered by Boxers. It was June 20. At 4 p.m. that afternoon, Imperial Chinese troops supported by Boxers started firing at the city's embassies, and the siege of Peking had begun.

The city's 900-odd foreigners, including around 400 soldiers from eight different countries, and 3,000 Chinese supporters, mostly Christian converts, withdrew to two defensive positions within the city.

Among the defenders was the Australian journalist George "Chinese" Morrison, who, after a celebrated career which included walking across Australia from north to south, established himself as an authority on eastern affairs, working as a correspondent for the London *Times* in China. Morrison's story of the siege was the first to reach the west.

Throughout the 55-day siege the defenders were heavily outnumbered by the Chinese. However, instead of quickly overwhelming the foreigners by massed assault, the Chinese Imperial troops wore down their adversaries with artillery fire, mining, and sniping, leaving direct assaults to the fanatical Boxers.

Allied troops and civilian troops defending their positions within the city walls were poorly equipped, each national unit possessing a different type of rifle, making the pooling of ammunition impossible. Ammunition supplies were also limited, to a maximum of 300 rounds per man. The defender's heaviest weapons were three pieces of artillery, one a five-barrelled Nordenfelt that jammed after every fourth shot, and a single machine-gun.

The foreigners were also greatly assisted by Chinese indecision. Tzu Hsi fluctuated between following the advice of a peace party and a war party and, perhaps influenced by the approach of a multi-national relief force, she imposed an unofficial two-week truce from July 15. It was then that the defenders first heard of the relief column.

Ironically, the British press had already reported that the legations had been overwhelmed and foreigners had been massacred, with the *Times* publishing an obituary for "Chinese" Morrison, who had, in fact, been wounded. The end came on August 14 when the allied armies entered the city and the defenders, by now reduced to eating horsemeat, came out from behind their barricades.

George Ernest Morrison

The French sector of Peking lies in ruins, bombarded by Chinese troops as the siege began.

Mounted on Chinese ponies, a small patrol of NSW sailors set out from Peking in February 1901 to mop up a handful of bandits. Mostly, however, the sailors found their last weeks in Peking very tedious.

them, playing and marching at a slower pace so that the pipers had to struggle to keep up and the Australians were constantly changing step, caught between the two kinds of music.

Inside the walled city of Peking there were smaller and older cities, themselves separately walled away. The Australians were split, a headquarters detachment of 96 men, including the Marine Light Infantry, in the Tartar City's Chang-wang Fu palace, 63 in the British Legation, just outside the Forbidden City, as guards, and another 64 posted to the Llama Temple, also on guard duties.

Like the Victorians, who had settled into quarters in Tientsin, the New South Welshmen began to notice that the weather had turned from chilly to cold. It was apparent to them that the British were making arrangements to move their troops out of China; some of the other internationals had already gone or were in the process of leaving; there were ominously snow-heavy clouds building and whatever Boxer hostility was still evident seemed likely to be low-level during the imminent winter.

It was November 1900, and the volunteer sailor-soldiers' lives were about to become rather more humdrum than they had expected. In a letter to the *Sydney Morning Herald* one of the Marines in Peking gave details of the daily timetable with night guard-duties "from tattoo to reveille with five or six rounds in the magazine, one in the chamber and a fixed bayonet. We rise at 6.30, roll call at 7, breakfast at 7.45, fall in at 9, dinner at 12.30, leave from 2 to 5.30, tea at 4.15, first post at 8.30, second at 9, lights out at 9.15pm."

The armed night-guard was there because of trouble still about on a small but potentially dangerous scale; the Australians dealt with it quickly, strictly and occasionally drastically. Flogging was a common punishment for a wide variety of lesser offences and, for major crimes and especially for taking up arms against the occupying powers, shooting was the expected thing. The Australians became used to forming firing-parties. In both Peking and Tientsin it was the most military duty they had.

Through Christmas 1900, through the parties to celebrate the season and the coming of the new year, through the ice and wind-chill of winter, the Naval Brigade acted as policemen, railwaymen, fire-fighters and soldier-guards all at once. They undertook the essential civil tasks of both cities, more, it can be assumed, because they were there and were told to than for any other reasons.

There was a fair amount of discontent among them, men and officers alike; they had been too late for military distinction or adventure and consequently too late for the successful looting which had gone on. The one expedition after loot which the Australians launched in consort with a party of Baluchi officers came to nothing other than the slaughter of 40 Boxers. The San Francisco *Chronicle* commented that the whole campaign to Peking had been "a carnival of loot. Stores, temples, palaces, hovels have been stripped of their stocks and furnishings by the avenging allied armies and there is not a soldier's haversack that is not weighted with Oriental treasure." The comment may have been correct for the American soldiers; the Australian sailors and Marines were not as well weighed down.

In March 1901, the entire Naval Brigade left China. They had fired their weapons, not in attack or defence, but only in retribution. They had lost some six men, but not to enemy action, only to sickness and injury. While they had been through a campaign of sorts and endured the bleak rigour of winter in northern China, thousands of their countrymen had been fighting in South Africa and earning an enviable reputation as soliders and a disreputable one in other ways. And while they were gone from home it had become a different place; the colonies had become a Commonwealth. And the old sovereign, Queen Victoria, was dead.

THE ELUSIVE BOER

"Fight for the land, brothers."

Invisible to approaching British infantry, Boer pickets in the niches of a rocky kopje guard the Pretoria railroad.

RIFLE-ARMED HORSEMEN OF THE WILDERNESS

The Boers fought a very different kind of war to what the mighty British Army was accustomed. Apart from their regular uniformed artillery men, the Boers did not have a standing army. Every *burgher* (male Boer farmer) between the ages of 16 and 60 was ready to fight and to provide his own horse, with a saddle and bridle, his own rifle and cartridges, and provisions for eight days out on the veldt. These volunteer citizen-soldiers on horseback were organised into highly mobile, well-armed guerrilla units called *commandos,* which varied in size from several hundred to several thousand men and came and went as the action demanded. The size of the irregular forces fluctuated; 65,000 Boers fought throughout the war, but there were never more than 35,000 in the field at any one time. Apart from the Artillery Corps and the South African Republic Police (ZARPs), the Boer forces wore no uniform; one war correspondent described a "motley-looking" group of fighters as "a crowd one is apt to see in a far inland shearing shed in Australia."

There was, however, nothing unsophisticated about the Boer force. The artillery, trained by German officers, had the most modern fieldguns, German Krupp and French Creusot batteries, which outranged British guns. Boer mounted infantrymen favoured the state-of-the-art German Mauser rifle, and Maxim machine-

A juggernaut on rails, this armoured locomotive carries Boer riflemen to protect the smaller engine and carriages behind it. The Boers derailed many British

A farmer acquaints himself with a Maxim machine-gun. The Boers fought with the best of European armaments.

supply trains as well as mining rail tracks, and the British also struck back at Boer railway transport in the same way.

Two Boer snipers make a bush camp near Ladysmith, using a primitive lean-to and a rocky outcrop for shelter.

Known to the British as the "Phantom of the Veldt", General Christiaan de Wet (hands crossed) stands with leaders of his commando. De Wet mastered guerilla warfare and harassed the British Army to the bitter end.

gun, and was a skilled marksman with both weapons. Invisibly entrenched behind boulders on rocky hills *(kopjes)* the Boer picked off advancing infantrymen with ease, often using small white stones left out on the plains as markers to judge his firing range. Lacking boulders for cover, the Boer built *sangars,* small protecting stone walls that blended with the rocky landscape. As the British infantry closed in, the Boers would leap on their ponies and disappear in a cloud of dust. The commandos continued to use these hit-and-run tactics throughout the war, avoiding, if possible, the set-piece battles employed by the British.

The Boer fighter had definite advantages over his British enemy. He had native horses in plentiful supply which were accustomed to an African climate and diet. He knew the country, and he had the majority of the population on his side. Fighting to defend his homeland, the Boer had few scruples about "honourable conduct", and British countermeasures only embittered and hardened the Boer who carried on the fight.

A Boer artillery unit assembles for attack. Such units complemented smaller ones specialising in lightning-fast raids and sabotage.

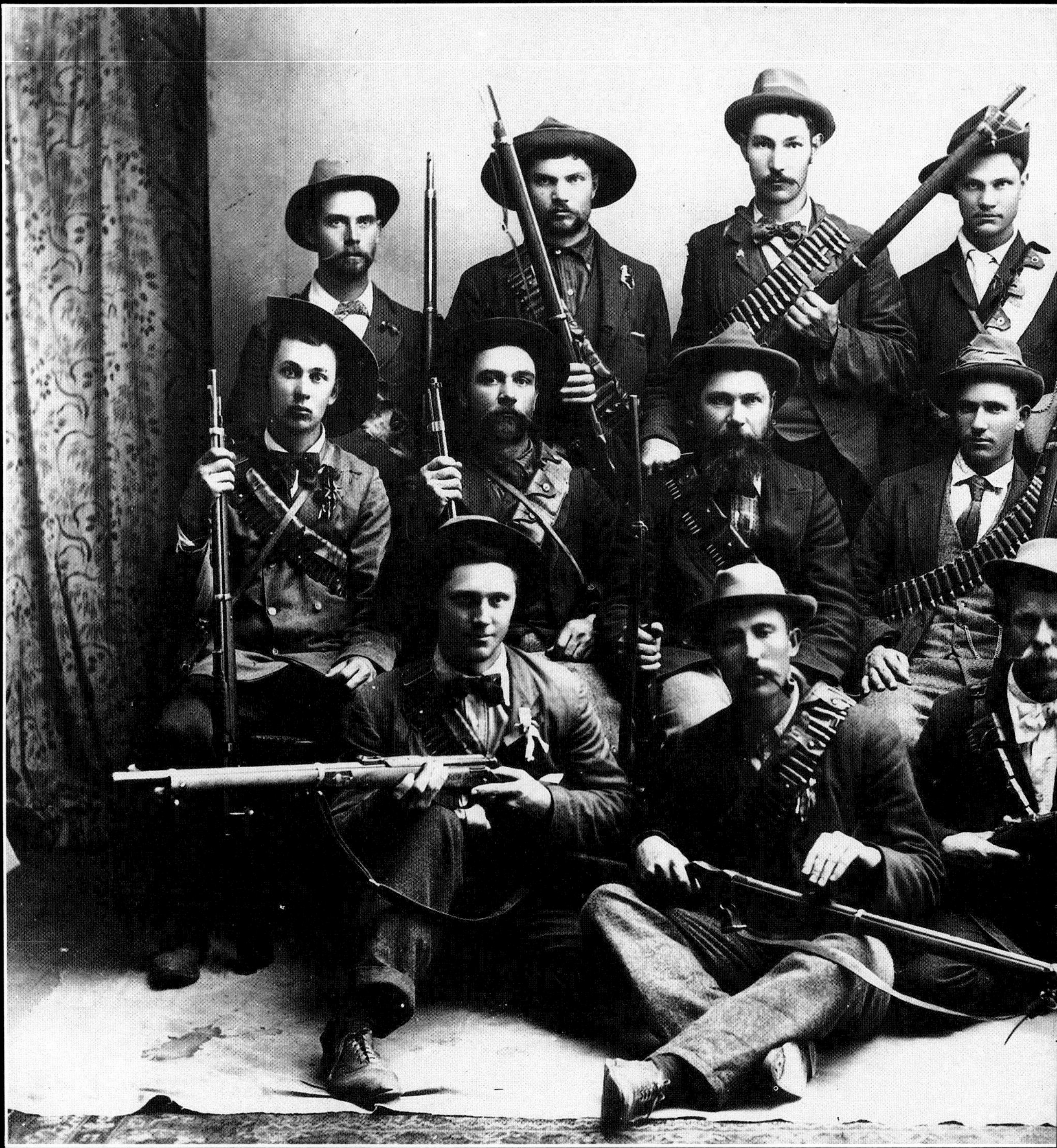

In their Sunday best with a medley of carbines and bandoliers, a Boer commandant and his men made a striking portrait of faith-inspired freedom-fighters.

Above: White-hatted General Louis Botha, and State Attorney Jan Smuts (left), glean intelligence from a Boer spy. Below: A Boer heliograph team use tripod-mounted reflectors to flash messages over great distances, as well as intercepting British heliograph transmissions.

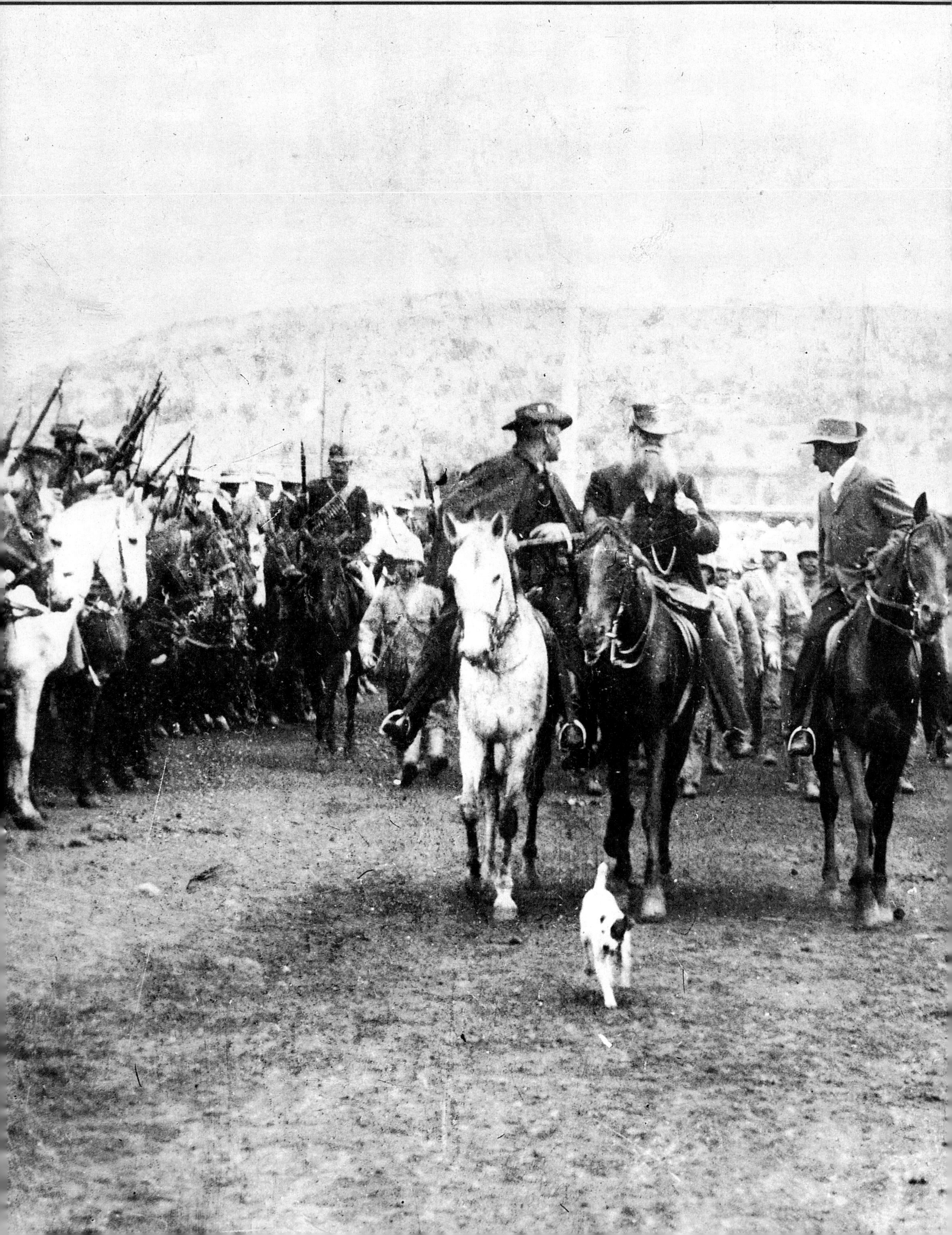

An armed guard of Boer horsemen flank British prisoners being led from Pretoria to a nearby P.O.W. camp.

4

THE TREK TO WAR

British and Boer forces had clashed in South Africa, and again Australia's colonies avidly sent troops for the Imperial cause. Then, in one black week, the fighting Boers showed their mettle and the war turned bad for Britain.

In the mid-1600s, a century-and-a-quarter before the first convicts dragged their leg-irons ashore on the coast of New South Wales, trading-posts were being built at the Cape of Good Hope. They were the Dutch East India Company's out-stations on the southern tip of Africa. And by the time Terra Australis had settled into its shackles as a penal settlement, the Cape was more than established; it had become rigid and inflexible.

Its original settlers had fled from religious persecution in their own countries. Word had come back to Europe of the initial opening-up of this new land and of its promise of freedom. So, to the Cape of Good Hope fled families from Holland and Germany and France — Protestants, Huguenots, Lutherans and Calvinists. All of them were believers in the fundamentalism of the Bible and in the prospect of finding another Eden in Africa.

They came close to it. They found a land in which the soil had barely been touched and which, for the turning and seeding, would yield full measure. They found good slopes where olives and lemons and grapes would grasp the earth and flourish. They found edible fruits and game in huge abundance, and a heavenly

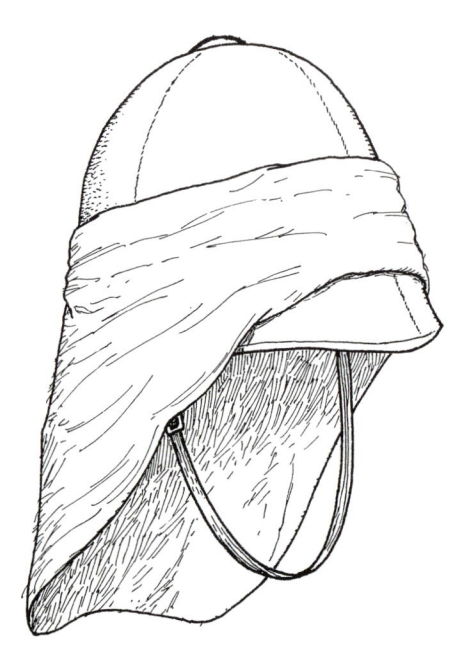

Foreign-service helmet of khaki cloth-covered cork, with neck protector. Worn by several British regiments in the Boer War.

balance between sunshine and rain. To make this honeyed life sweeter, there were black men to serve them.

There was, of course, a serpent. It was a short, stocky man called Napoleon Bonaparte, and his actions swept tidal waves of reactions across the world. French influence was already strong in Indo-China, northern Africa and India itself, its ships posing a potential threat along the trade routes to the Far East. Britain, which had professed no interest at all in the settlement at the Cape, suddenly realised that it offered a perfect naval base and safe port for British ships to and from New Zealand, Australia and the treasure-house of India. So, with the chill indifference of the world's dominant power, Britain annexed the Cape in 1806. It was a deft political action; a simple theft by force.

The incursion of the British into South Africa produced a split between them and the now long-settled Afrikaners. There were already the differences in language; the farmers — the local word was Boer — spoke Afrikaans, a version of Dutch, but the laws and policies were made and written in English. In 1834, one such law forbade slavery in any part of the British Empire, and that included the Cape Colony.

The split became a rift at once. There were Boer families and, indeed, whole communities, who felt that they could no longer live under this British yoke which had annexed their ancestral lands, flouted the Bible's absolute word, and now taken from them their working slaves. They determined to move out, to head north into the heart of Africa, unaware or uncaring that any such move was an invasion of tribal lands. So began the Great Trek, not as long as the Israelites' desert wandering, but lasting in all until 1852. In those 16 years, the greatly-laden Cape carts lumbered across the Orange River, tailed by strings of cattle and horses, hung about with boxes of poultry, led and driven by the stern and fiercely independent Boers. They founded the Orange Free State, and some of them went north again across the Vaal River to found the republic of the Transvaal. They were free people again, free to farm, to hunt, to pray as they wished and to own slaves. And free of the British.

Britain was very understanding about it all. The people who had gone had been potential trouble-makers; better that they should go and live in the wilderness. Britain had enough on her hands at the time, in particular, a long-running conflict with the Kaffir tribes, a web of natives spread across southern Africa, speakers of the Bantu tongue, and normally peaceful herdsmen and hunters. They resented the incursion of the white man and made little distinction between the Dutch and the British. Britain's Redcoats, however, often found themselves in skirmishes, punitive expeditions, and large-scale engagements with the Kaffirs.

The tribes succeeded only in bringing about the deaths of more than two thirds of their own interlinked people and the loss of all their territory. While their enemies had been British in the broad sense, there had also been local volunteers of all kinds, including Boers. For the British it was simply a good tactic to keep the Boers onside in the struggle with the Kaffirs, and quite early in the fighting, in 1852, Britain gave up its Transvaal region and recognised an independent South African Republic. Two years later, while still pitched against the natives, there came the recognised independence of the Orange Free State.

Then, for a dozen years it was all war of one small, deadly kind or another. The proud warriors who called themselves amaZulu, the People of Heaven, fought the Boers along their borders and fought among themselves and looked towards fighting the British. In Basutoland, that warrior tribe hit back hard at Boer inroads into its land after the Boers had tried the British tactic of annexation. The fighting increased until the British themselves annexed the whole of Basutoland, including what the Boers had taken. The Boers also began to fight among themselves and it took the strongest efforts of the South African Republic's first president, Marthinus Pretorius, and his principal aide, Paul Kruger, to prevent insurgency and civil war.

Boer farmers established a homeland in South Africa from the mid-17th century, but by the mid-1800s Britain's presence there conflicted with Boer claims to the country. After Britain annexed the Cape Colony and Natal, the Boers fled northwards, crossing the Orange River to form the independent Orange Free State. Still more Boers went further, across the Vaal River to form the South African Republic, known as the Transvaal. Outnumbered by native blacks and white immigrants, the Boers struggled to maintain supremacy within their new borders (marked grey), which weren't respected by the British, who had occupied most of southern and eastern South Africa (marked pink). Diplomatic negotiations failed, as British forces raided into Transvaal, and a Boer ultimatum to the British in October 1899 led to war.

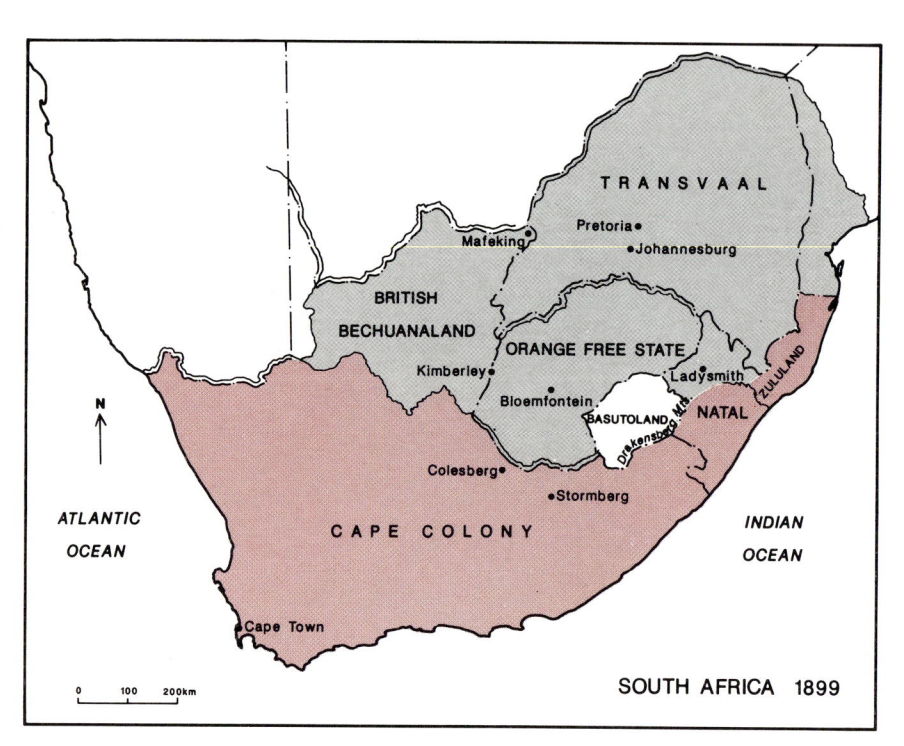

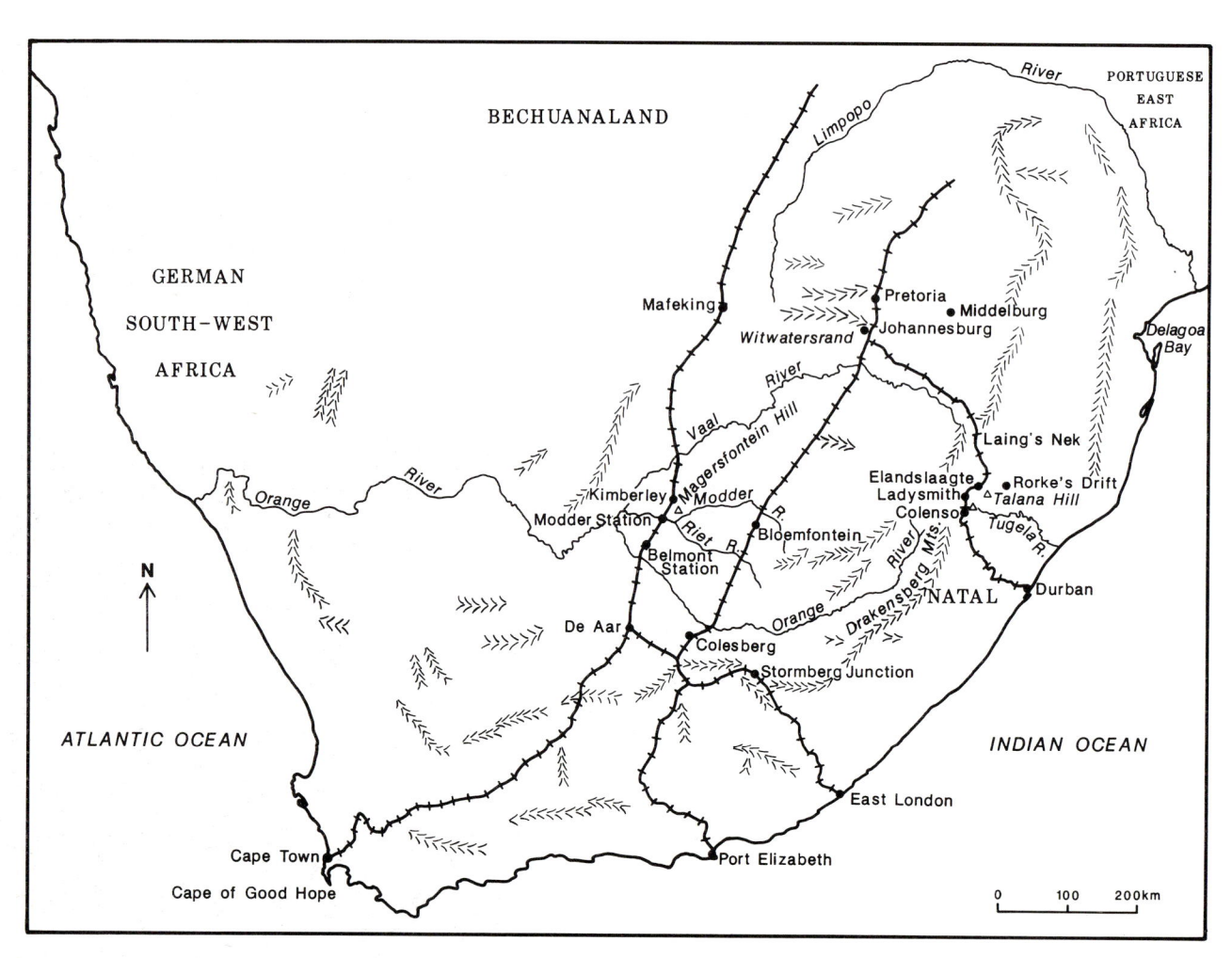

SOUTH AFRICA 1899

All of this simmered in the African sun, a vast pot of trouble brewing, occasionally bubbling to the rim, never quite spilling right over. And then the heat went up in 1867 with the discovery of a pipe of diamonds at Kimberley, along the Orange River. Where there was likely to be great profit, Britain soon made her presence felt. In 1872 she annexed the diamond-bearing region, re-annexed it in fact, from the Orange Free State, despite roars of outrage and protest.

Five years later, in 1877, Britain annexed the recognised and independent South African Republic, the Transvaal. The political reasoning behind the move was a sort of deck-clearing action in readiness for the unification of all of South Africa into a federation, and in preparation for a war which was plainly coming with the Zulus.

Eight months in 1879 saw it begin and end. The Zulu War left more than 2,000 British troops and native followers slaughtered at Isandhlwana, and saw the extraordinary defence of Rorke's Drift by 85 British soldiers against several thousand blood-hungry Zulus. It also saw the death in action of a young French volunteer, Louis Napoleon, Prince Imperial and son of Napoleon III, and if it did nothing else, the young man's death focused international attention on Britain's actions in South Africa, a focus which sharpened when the Zulu power was smashed and Britain once again stood triumphant over "native rebels".

It was now back to Britain versus the Boers: a straight, two-way contest. And it began disastrously for the British, who listed it as the Transvaal Revolt. South Africans would later call it the first Anglo-Boer war, but, by any name, it was a calamity for Britain.

When the Boer Republic was proclaimed on December 30, 1880, several small units of British troops were cut up or imprisoned. Exactly four weeks later, Boer leader Piet Joubert took a 2,000-man invasion force into the British-annexed Natal, confronted the British General, Sir George Colley, at Laing's Nek in the Drakensberg Mountains, and defeated his garrison army resoundingly, although Colley got away. A month later again, his lesson unlearned, Colley split the forces he had and took 550 men up to the crest of the Majuba Hill, overlooking a pass. He seems not to have considered that he was himself overlooked by Boer marksmen and it cost him dearly. Half his men managed to get away; 59 became unwounded prisoners and 134 were wounded. Ninety-two were killed, General Colley among them. Boer casualties were negligible.

These were grim lessons for Britain and led its government to sign the Treaty of Pretoria, which granted independence to the Republic of South Africa — under British sovereign power. Paul Kruger, the dour, grim advocate of complete Boer independence, became the Republic's president. It was April 5, 1883, and there were yet to be 16 years of what had come to seem like ordinary African events.

British troops fought the Matabele and Mashona nations, and the Zulus once more, and performed again the old geopolitical trick of annexing Zululand. Germany established a colony in south-west Africa, emphasising the enclosure of the Boers, who now had native tribes and other nations to their north and west, and Britain to their south and east. And more riches were discovered: a great seam of gold in the Witwatersrand.

Suddenly the Boers had an internationally recognised Republic which was about to become one of the world's richest lands. Between its gold and the Orange Free State's diamonds, between Kimberley and what became known as the Rand, there lay the key to world economics. With that realisation came three others: Britain's annexation of Zululand and Natal effectively blocked the Boer republics from the sea, except through another nation's territory; led by Cecil Rhodes, millionaire-miner-entrepreneur and Prime Minister of Cape Colony, there were strong moves to bring the whole of southern Africa under British domination; and the gold of the Rand had brought miners from all over the world, but predominantly from the white British Empire, into South Africa.

Kruger and his people were in a double

Well exposed, colourful targets, a large British force sweeps across a ridge in Natal during the first Boer War. The British had bitter lessons to learn abou

fighting a stealthy and well camouflaged foe.

minority. Not only were there more blacks by the millions, but there were suddenly thousands more whites. And those white miners were *Uitlanders,* foreigners, with no rights and no votes, but with loud voices demanding both. Kruger, determined on independence from Britain, was equally determined that the *Uitlanders* should not be given voting rights, but he continued to tax them, and that did nothing to lower the temperature internally.

Externally, it had become common knowledge that Kruger had been using massive amounts of the seemingly endless Rand gold to buy arms from Germany and France. He also had plans for a railroad to run into Portuguese East Africa and so breach the wall Britain had built around him.

Kruger's unflinching attitudes, especially towards votes for *Uitlanders* led to more and more discontent among those taxed but not represented, and a growing body of "reformers" began to build. There was talk of an uprising.

Rhodes, alive to the possibilities, quietly supported the reformers and watched and waited as secret stocks of arms and ammunition were made ready in Johannesburg. He ordered Dr. Leander Starr Jameson, administrator of the British South Africa Company and its private army, to prepare a mounted force of 800 volunteer troopers and hold them on standby in Mafeking, in north-western Cape Colony. His orders were to be ready to ride in to Johannesburg if the reformers rose against the Kruger government.

On New Year's Day, 1896, a shocked world learned that Dr. Jameson was riding into the Transvaal to take armed support to the *Uitlanders,* who had, he maintained, written asking for help. The unsigned letter was later proved to be fraudulent. What was real was his readiness to ride, his cutting of the telegraph wires behind him so that no recall could reach him from Rhodes, and his gross error in assuming that his presence would provoke an uprising. In the event, the reformers made a weak display and then surrendered and Jameson and his 800 were captured by the first Boer troops who confronted them.

The Jameson raid added strength to Kruger's position, both in his own land and abroad. Ger-

THE BRITISH BLUNDERER

Descended on his mother's side from the Earl Marshals of England, Sir Redvers Buller was brought up to luxury and wealth. Even as a cavalry subaltern he displayed a solid frame around a well-filled stomach, but he also showed a good seat on a horse and, by the time of the Boer War, an enviable military reputation. He had fought in five campaigns, earned the Victoria Cross in the Zulu War and formed the Army Service Corps in 1888. He was given overall command in South Africa at the age of 60, with no qualifications for the task other than his undoubted bravery: he had never commanded a large body of troops in the field and went to South Africa after 10 years of desk service. He was to face a most elusive foe.

Buller quickly showed his style by scrapping the War Office plan of an advance on the Boer republics and decided instead to split his forces into three columns, leaving the Cape Colony largely undefended. The tragic result was Black Week, in December 1899, the few days in which the British were thrashed at Stormberg, Magersfontein and Colenso.

London's immediate response was to send out Lord Roberts to take command, with Kitchener as his chief of staff. Buller, always considerate of his troops' welfare, was a very popular commander, but his popularity could not outweigh his general lack of success in the field, his indecision and lack of self-confidence, nor his occasional studied indifference to orders. He was sent home in January 1900 and resumed the Aldershot command he had held a year earlier.

Then, in the wake of the uproar caused by his defence of his actions in advising the surrender of Ladysmith, he was dismissed and retired to live in the country till his death in 1908.

Sir Redvers Buller was responsible for so many British disasters in the Boer War that he was nicknamed "Sir Reverse".

many's Kaiser Wilhelm sent a telegram of congratulation and, in 1898, Kruger was re-elected with a massive majority. In that same year, Britain's new representative at the Cape, Sir Alfred Milner, arrived and despite his announced opposition to what he called "Krugerism", he and the Boer leader met to confer in Bloemfontein in May 1899.

Kruger made some concessions and permitted voting rights to *Uitlanders* who fulfilled certain residential requirements. Milner maintained that this was not enough. Kruger conceded further, but again Milner demanded more; he wanted all *Uitlander* grievances settled before any agreement could be reached.

A trim young lawyer in the Cape Colony wrote later: "It became so clear to me that the British connection was harmful to South Africa's best interests that I feared my future position as a Cape politician would be a false one. I therefore left the Old Colony for good." He moved quickly to the Transvaal and there became Kruger's state attorney. His name was Jan Smuts and, when Britain began to move troops from the Cape to the Transvaal border and ordered reinforcements from India, Smuts wrote the Boer ultimatum.

The ultimatum uncomprisingly accused Britain of interfering in the internal affairs of the Transvaal and of massing troops in a way that threatened that state. It demanded arbitration on all points of difference, withdrawal of British troops on the Republic's borders, and of all British reinforcements which had arrived in South Africa after June 1, and that any troops already on their way to South Africa were not to land. Smuts wound up the maxim by stating quite politely, "That unless Her Majesty's Government complies within 48 hours the government of the South African Republic (Transvaal) would with great regret be compelled to regard the action as a formal declaration of war."

The ultimatum was not sent for 10 days, days spent ensuring that, if war should come, the Orange Free State would stand with their Boer brothers in the Republic of South Africa. The Free State's president, Marthinus Steyn, refused to rush his decision, his interim reply stating firmly, "The day I say war it will be war to the bitter end."

THE RELUCTANT PATRIOT

Like Kruger, Piet Joubert was a child of the Great Trek. Unlike Kruger he was a townsman, a well-dressed and well-spoken businessman, as fluent in English as in the Taal, the African-Dutch Boer tongue. He had investments in land, houses and gold shares and was runner-up in three presidential elections. As a soldier he had defeated the British at Majuba Hill in 1881, and in 1899 he led the progressives in the parliament, opposing the ideas of war.

Yet when the war began, he became Commandant-General and certainly he looked the part, flashing eyes above a flowing beard and a manner which exuded confidence. Much of that was a facade. He was continually wracked by the thought that the war was unnecessary and the ill-feeling between himself and Kruger did little to help. Nonetheless he fought well in the first year of the war but at the end of 1899, old and unwell, worried by supply shortages and continuous disputes with Kruger, he received massive internal injuries after being thrown from his horse, and later died. massive internal injuries.

Commandant-General Piet Joubert (centre with hat on knee), chief of the Boer forces, leads a commando near Modderspruit.

President Kruger, Oom (Uncle) Paul to his followers, negotiated hard for total independence from Britain, yet armed the Boer Republic for war.

Meanwhile, Kruger beat back such opposition as there was in his parliament, then on October 9, 1899, Steyn agreed to stand by the Transvaal, and the ultimatum was sent. Kruger and Steyn both knew that Britain neither would or could accept its terms, and indeed the phrase which Cabinet used was that those terms "were impossible to discuss". It was over the brink and into war.

Only a matter of days passed before the main thrust began. General Piet Cronje led his troops out of Transvaal, east across the border and to the town of Mafeking, besieging it on October 14. A day later Orange Free State forces in the south locked diamond-rich Kimberley into a siege. But it was when General Piet Joubert led 15,000 men in a swinging arc round the Drakensberg Mountains in the east and fought a series of engagements on the march that the country was plunged into a total state of hostility. He had first pushed through Lieutenant-General Sir George White's Natal Defence Force at Laing's Nek on October 12, then a week later brushed them aside at Talana Hill. White held them in check at Elandslaagte the next day long enough for his advanced brigade to withdraw into Ladysmith, but that check did no more than make the Boers pause in their inexorable move on Ladysmith. The siege closed on that city on November 2 and completed a trio of investments — Mafeking to the north, Kimberley to the west, and Ladysmith to the east. The war was scarcely a month old and the Boers had drawn first blood.

Britain was out-gunned and out-manned, and though it was generally out of favour with the rest of the world because of its bullying tactics against the independent states of South Africa, it still had the Empire's colonies and dominions on which to call. Even as early as July 1899, when it first seemed as though diplomacy and dialogue in South Africa were going to yield to an outbreak at arms, an almost over-eager Queensland colonial government offered to send 250 mounted infantry with machine-guns if war should be declared. The offer was matched at once by the governments of NSW and Victoria. Then in September that year, before any declaration of war, a joint conference of Australian colonial military commandants agreed to offer Britain a contingent of 2,500 troops — cavalry, infantry, mounted infantry and artillery.

In London, the War Office had no perception of the worth of these colonial troops so freely offered, choosing to consider them as less than first-rate and certainly not as skilled or reliable as British regulars. The British Government, however, saw the offer in a rather different light. There had been growing unfavourable comment — in America and much of Europe, in particular, Germany — about Britain's actions in South Africa. While the War Office's first reaction was to send a carefully worded and properly grateful refusal, the government's demands for an overt show of Empire unity took precedence. Under cabinet-room pressure, the War Office accepted the offer from the Australian colonies, be it in its own strict and hidebound fashion.

One Australian detachment, however, had no need to wait for the call. The NSW Lancers, a volunteer regiment with a sound tradition of paying its own way, had raised money to send men to Britain to take part in military tournaments and to attend and parade at the 1897 celebrations for Queen Victoria's Diamond Jubilee. They were successful and popular participants, and in 1899 they sent a squadron of 72 men under Captain (later General) Charles Cox for training with the British Cavalry. The Boer war began as they were readying to return to Australia and on their homeward journey they virtually jumped ship at Cape Town and offered themselves for service. One troop was attached to the 9th Lancers for a short while and became known as "the fighting twenty-nine"; then they rejoined the rest of Captain Cox's command which formed an extra squadron within the 6th Inniskilling Dragoons.

They landed in South Africa less than a month after the first troops from Australia stepped ashore at Cape Town. That had been on the last day of October, 1899, not long after their newly appointed commander-in-chief, General Sir Redvers Buller. And more troopships were already on the way from Australia with volunteers who had rushed to join the Colours in a wild desire to get to the war before the fighting finished. There were also Australians living and

Under Queen Victoria's benign gaze, soldiers bound for South Africa enjoy a gala luncheon in their honour at the Exhibition Building in Adelaide, before embarking on active service.

working in South Africa, and they enlisted too; one of Buller's units was the Imperial Light Horse of South Africa, raised by Walter Karri-Davies, a Broken Hill man who found his recruits among the Australians working around him in the goldfields near Johannesburg. Buller was to have other Empire troops under his command as well: the first of 10 shiploads of New Zealanders was on the water and a contingent from Canada was being fitted out to sail. And there was an Army Corps of 47,000 from Britain disembarking behind him.

The man these colonials and regulars would serve was a bluff, hearty soldier, a veteran of several African campaigns — against the Ashanti, the first Boer War from 1880 to 1881, and against the Zulu, a campaign from which he emerged with a Victoria Cross. He was jovial and popular with the troops, but he had never handled large formations in battle and, in his sixties, he had not kept pace with new military developments nor did he place much reliance

MAFEKING: BADEN-POWELL'S TRIUMPH

It might well have been called the war of three sieges. On October 14, 1899, three days after war was declared, the Boer general Piet Cronje laid siege to Mafeking. A day later, Kimberley, diamond heart of the world, was locked in by Orange Free State forces, and a fortnight later again, on November 2, General Piet Joubert's army forced Lieutenant-General Sir George White to withdraw into Ladysmith where his 12,000 men were bottled up away from the open war.

The three towns formed a triangle — Kimberley and Ladysmith at the base, Mafeking to the north — and, in common, they shared the strategic fact of being in British territory, attacked and besieged by border-crossing Boers. Ladysmith was useful to the Boers because they were able to hold a large force there. Kimberley was a splendid coup for them since they tied up the diamond mines and their output. But Mafeking seemed so pointless that British officer, Lieutenant-Colonel Sir Hubert Plumer, asked, "Why would a cavalry officer dig-in to hold a shanty-town as soon as the first shot was fired?"

The cavalry officer in question was unlikely to run away from an enemy force. Robert Stephenson Smyth Baden-Powell, a Londoner, educated at Charterhouse School, had joined the army in 1876 and had served in India and Afghanistan before Africa. He had been chief of staff in Rhodesia before the war and had been seen as a coming man, although there were reservations about his style. He was prepared to throw the book away and make his own rules when it suited him. He was considered to be callous to a marked degree, especially after he had answered accusations that he had murdered an African chieftain, commenting that the dead man had deserved it.

As a counter-balance to his reputation as an opportunist, he was a natural leader and a fine field soldier with no lack of courage. When the Boers began their assault on Mafeking he organised a well-planned defence and prepared to fight. He had little with which to oppose the investing force of more than 5,000 Boers; under command he had 20 officers and 700 men of a newly-raised unit, the Protectorate Regiment, some police and about 300 armed townsmen, and they were expected to hold a 10-kilometre perimeter.

Baden-Powell, already well-known as "BP", took total control of the garrison and began to improvise in his leadership. The artillery was a mixed battery of small-calibre guns the best of which were two ancient muzzle-loading 7-pounders; to supplement these the besieged men came up with bomb-throwing devices and grenades with which to load them. And a narrow-gauge railway was built with-

With no natural defences, the sprawling city of Mafeking proved difficult to hold against a vastly superior force.

on field intelligence. He was also somewhat given to getting flustered in the face of crisis.

His orders were plain. He was to launch an attack at once from the Cape, using the railway from De Aar to Bloemfontein. With most of the Boers involved in the three sieges, the line and the country round it could have been taken easily. The Boer forces would have been drawn to him at points of his choosing and at the same time the sieges would have been weakened or lifted.

Buller chose not to do that. He decided, most unwisely, to split his army and try dealing with the three most immediate enemy threats at once. He sent his 1st Division under Lieutenant-General Lord Methuen to advance from the western Cape to relieve Kimberley. He took most of the remainder of his troops by sea to Durban and then along the railway line to the edge of a wide plain where he camped; beyond the plain was the Tugela River, the small town of Colenso and then Ladysmith. And because

in the town to move supplies, men and ammunition quickly. Baden-Powell supervised everything, including the heavily stockpiled rations, but his supervision was deeply racist.

Within the perimeter was a native enclave sheltering 8,000 Africans. The unusual step was taken of arming 300 of them and giving them a section of perimeter to guard; the rest he used unmercifully as labour-gangs, making them dig the town's defences and repair damage from the constant bombardment in return for a miserly ration. He then changed the rations for Africans to exclude wheat and corn and to include oats and other grains and grasses meant for horses.

In January BP made the decision to offer the town's African refugees the cruel choice of staying and starving, because he would feed them no longer, or going out onto the veldt and risking Boer fire. Hundreds of them, staggered gauntly away from the defences they had dug. How many died, no one knows.

Even so, BP's initials were on everyone's lips. The bright and determined, yet impetuous and callous colonel was to become a nation's hero, people ignoring his stated pleasure that a bit of "nigger hunting was good sport".

The seven-month siege was lifted on May 17, 1900, by a flying column of cavalry and mounted infantry under Colonel Bryan Mahon; they had ridden 380 kilometres from the Vaal River in 12 days through rough terrain and a Boer army. News of their arrival and of Mafeking's relief brought a wave of hysteria to Britain, and wild scenes of jubilation and excitement were witnessed in London's streets. The name of the town became a part of the English language; dictionaries show the word "mafficking" as meaning "the celebration of a national victory with great demonstrations of joy".

Baden-Powell continued to serve during the war, heading a relief column that failed to relieve a unit of Australians trapped at a camp at Elands River in August 1900 because he did not scout ahead properly. He left the army as a major-general in 1907 to found the Boy Scouts movement, the international organisation based on the cadet corps he had raised in Mafeking, using young lads as messengers. In 1909, with his sister Agnes, he founded the Girl Guides and, knighted for these works, he died full of honours in 1941.

Colonel Robert Baden-Powell.

there was a formidable Boer force raiding in Cape Colony, Buller saw fit to break off a brigade under Major-General Sir William Gatacre to deal with it. Mafeking was considered less than vital at this stage, and was left to hold out on its own.

The NSW Lancers were still with Britain's 9th Lancers as part of Lord Methuen's cavalry screen, in a column of close to 10,000 men and 16 guns. They were in time for the first real battle, a grim overture to a season of tragedy, itself preceded by a series of short dramas. As the column moved northwards heading for Kimberley, there was brisk fighting in which the Lancers, on reconnaissance with some mounted infantry, were under considerable fire and were forced to withdraw. That was on November 10. They rode and exchanged fire through to the 23rd, when there was strong fighting on rising ground near Belmont Station and at Enslin. Veteran campaigners from the Guards Brigade and the Northumberland Fusiliers, supported by Royal Marines and seamen from the Naval Brigade, engaged in the sort of old-fashioned tactics which made them easy meat for the Boer guns.

One British point of view, however, saw the action differently: "Boldly advancing against the flaming bastions of stone and steel, the Northumberland Fusiliers and the Grenadiers led the way and rushed the Boers' first line. The enemy did not wait for the bayonets of the Grenadiers. With deadly earnestness a second kopje was stormed, then came a third hill and here the Boers made a desperate and determined stand. As our men went up they received them with a terrible and withering fire, before which down went officer after officer, down went many a brave man of humbler rank. Undismayed, however, the survivors pressed on and finally rushed in with the bayonet. Had

THE DIAMOND KING

Cecil John Rhodes was born to a Hertfordshire clergyman's wife in 1853 and grew into a young man so poor in health that it was considered unwise for him to go to university. Instead he went to join his older brother, a planter, in Natal. Once there, his health improved, and he moved to Kimberley to work in the diamond mines, making a fortune in two years. But all the time, he dreamed of a southern Africa consolidated into one state under the British crown.

In 1876, Rhodes resumed his education, at the same time drawing most of Kimberley's diamond mines into one company, De Beers Consolidated Mines. By 1881 he controlled almost all of the world's output of diamonds, and in that year he took another step toward his dream; he was elected to the Assembly of the Cape Colony and at once began his campaign to advance British authority in Africa, seeking more land, more wealth, and more control. He was influential in the annexation of Bechuanaland (now Botswana) and in the forced surrender by the Matabele of their homeland. That great and rich territory — now Zambia — became known then as Rhodesia.

The charter to administer and develop these new areas which lay along the northern edge of the Transvaal, one of the two independent Boer states, went to the British South Africa Company, with Rhodes at its head. He was joined by his close friend, Scottish doctor Leander Starr Jameson, who looked after the "administrative" duties that included the company's police force. In 1890, Rhodes became Premier of the Cape Colony and was in a strong enough political position — and certainly a wealthy enough one — to introduce his plan for the Cape-to-Cairo railroad, an essential step towards his vision of a united Africa.

After the siege of Kimberley, Rhodes stole the credit for the town's defence from the quietly efficient garrison commander, Lieutenant-Colonel Robert Kekewich. During the siege Rhodes had produced plenty of drama by using deep diamond mineshafts to shelter women and children from constant Boer bombardment. He did not seem to worry that there was no sanitation or proper ventilation in the shafts.

Rhodes died of tuberculosis in 1902, aged 49, but his best known achievement came about after his death. He had left provision in his will for the founding and maintenance of one of the world's great academic bounties, the Rhodes Scholarships.

cavalry been at hand in force to pursue, the victory would have been a decisive one. The infantry displayed a spirit equal to any ever displayed in the field, never flinching from the hail of bullets but cheering bravely while ever pressing forward. The Scots Guards went into action with pipes playing all the while."

The same account implied that enemy casualties were far higher than the few found, suggesting that the Boers either "carried them off as usual or stuffed them away into deftly constructed utility graves and cupboards of stone." As well, it says the British lost about 220 men, and makes the first mention of a lack of "fair play", telling of Boers showing a white flag and then firing as they were approached, of wounded Boers firing on those offering aid and of the use of the infamous dum-dum bullet. Such comments were the first itching signs of what would become a festering sore.

On the morning of November 28, Lord Methuen moved his forces forward again. He outnumbered the Boers by about three to two, but he was moving into their carefully determined territory. He was also faced by two Boer generals of considerable tactical guile, Cronje and Koos De la Rey. The British force, now with some New Zealanders, Canadians and Cape Colony detachments, faced a wide stretch of open country before they could reach the crossing points of the Modder River and the way beyond to Kimberley.

The Boers had dug rifle pits along the line of the river, on the near side, the side of the advance. De la Rey had "decorated" the forward area of the plain with empty tins and marked and painted rocks; each of them was a known ranging-point for both riflemen and gunners. When the advance began, the attack was allowed to get well into the river's loop before the

Mounted troops water their horses at the Orange River. Long treks across the hot, dry veldt with no natural cover characterised this war.

Boer artillerymen change the bearings on the 94-pounder Creusot "Long Tom" to bombard the besieged city of Mafeking in December 1899. The Boer

commander, General Piet Cronje, had nine other modern field-guns at his disposal.

Never short of a story, Boer war correspondents keep a close eye on the battle.

PATERSON AND THE PRESS

There have always been chroniclers of war. As far back as Josephus and Xenophon and Gaius Julius Caesar, there have been a multitude of on-the-spot stories, reports and comments from such at-the-time soldiers or observers. Yet it was not until the Crimean War that the war correspondent came into being, an official, accredited observer/reporter, not a soldier but moving and living with soldiers; not a commander but with access to command decision-making; a man without weapons but still vulnerable to the hazards of combat.

The first war correspondent was William Howard Russell of *The Times*, a man whose probing eye and righteous pen brought home to the people of Britain the horror, futility and incompetence of the Crimean campaign, as well as the simple, unthinking bravery of the British soldier.

By the time of the Boer war, the war correspondent was an established figure and newspapers sought to buy the services of well-known names, whether they had any journalistic or military experience or not. The campaigning in South Africa was well covered by reporters and authors. Among them was the young Winston Churchill; Bennett Burleigh of the *Daily Telegraph*, whose aide was "Breaker" Morant; Rudyard Kipling who set up a newspaper for the troops; Edgar Wallace who sent back a series of articles which later made a book called *Unofficial Dispatches*. And, from Australia, the man who was known and loved as "The Banjo" — Andrew Barton Paterson.

By the time he landed at the Cape as war correspondent for the *Sydney Morning Herald*, Banjo Paterson was already a national literary figure, "The Man from Snowy River" and "Clancy of the Overflow" to his name. As a reporter he was to see the Australian bushmen he knew so well in a different and more dangerous light. He accompanied the NSW Lancers on their long treks, rode with dispatches through Boer-occupied country and was the first correspondent into Bloemfontein, and he wrote of it all with a humour and clarity which earned him the praise of his editor, his public and other pressmen. The Reuters News Agency was so impressed with Paterson that he was appointed as their special correspondent with the Australian and New Zealand forces.

He was a man from the country and delighted in the South African veldt, some of it as harsh and unfeeling as the gibber and scrub country of Australia, some of it lush. He wrote: "We pushed on through the open veldt, the long grass brushing the horses' knees and forming a dense carpet under their feet. This is the most wonderful grassed country I have ever seen."

For Paterson the grass meant fodder; he was a horseman and a lover of horses and his writing echoed that feeling as it resounded with his strong nationalism. "The big English horses of the Scots Greys do not stand up to the conditions anywhere near as well as our wiry Australian Walers; gun-horses drop in their harness and pistol-shots constantly mark the sad end of their misery."

And, linking horse and man, he wrote, "The greatest qualities needed for the troops were mobility, dash and intelligence, and in all these qualities the Australian and New Zealand regiments without exception proved their excellence. The Australians were accustomed all their lives to finding their way in the open, to noticing what was taking place around them and to relying on themselves at a pinch; the English 'Tommies' were drilled and trained to obey orders, and there their ideas stopped."

In Africa, in the war against the Boers, Banjo Paterson broadened his personal experience of men and events and, through his articles and verse and later books, offered some new perspectives to his readers. And he set the stage for other Australians who were to record history — for Keith Murdoch who broke the Gallipoli story, for Alan Moorehead and Chester Wilmot in World War II, and for the reporters, men and women, who went "with our forces at the Front" in Malaya and Korea and Vietnam.

cannonading from the far side began, the marksmen in the trenches rising only just enough to fire into the solidly massed formations approaching them. The Highlanders' pipes soon squealed and whimpered into an awful silence.

Firing as they were from ground level and at close range, the Boer riflemen were agonisingly effective; a bullet striking flesh would pass through, tumbling and yawing to wound a second man, perhaps a third. A bullet striking bone would distort and ricochet, still a missile and now possibly carrying with it bone fragments as secondary missiles. There were some terrible wounds from rifle fire and from the more impersonal gunnery. Worse was the fact that the enemy could not be seen, his positions so well selected that Methuen could not outflank him, though the Australians and other mounted troops did try. On top of that the wounded had to lie out there, motionless, through a long day of death.

Blood had to be left to seep into the sandy ground till it closed a wound, or till it ceased to flow for ever. Thirst and the stinging tickle of ants had to be endured, for any move which showed above the level of the coarse scrub drew a hail of Boer bullets. And the sun shone without mercy, drying sweat-soaked uniforms to a crackle of cloth and baking the skin beneath. For the Highlanders, bare to the buttocks beneath their kilts, that searing heat was an added savagery in an already inhuman day.

There was no further advance until dark, and then only with caution and only to succour the wounded. One of Methuen's regimental officers wrote in a letter home: "We had to keep our position all night with not a soul near us and nothing to eat and drink. Our orders were to open fire as soon as it was light enough, and the infantry were to take the place at the point of the bayonet. But in the morning the Boers had fled. The field presented a terrible sight at daybreak; there were dead and dying in every direction. We lost heavily on our side but the Boer losses must have been heavier. They bury their dead in their trenches as soon as they drop so that one cannot gauge their loss, but we counted hundreds." That was not quite correct. Methuen's losses were 72 killed and 396 wounded. Boer casualties were negligible.

Between that Boer withdrawal on November 28 and December 7, Methuen established a headquarters in the pleasant little village of Modder, took reinforcements and supplies and set up strongpoints and artillery positions along the whole line of the Modder River, where the Boers had previously sat. Among his reinforcements were a number of Canadian detachments and the first contingent of Victorian Mounted Rifles to join the NSW Lancers, who were screening a battery of Royal Horse Artillery.

The Australian poet, writer and war correspondent, A. B. "Banjo" Paterson, had not been much impressed with the quality of the troops with whom he had travelled out to the Cape. He considered them immature and felt there was too much rivalry and squabbling among them. Yet by the time he reached Modder River, he had changed his opinion enough to write that they "looked more smart and wide-awake than the English." There were others of those smart and wide-awake colonials on the way: the Queensland Mounted Infantry were disembarking and being organised to go by train to Orange River to hold the line there. They were in position for the beginning of a very black week.

Major-General Gatacre who, with a diminished brigade had been sent off to chase the raiders in Cape Colony, finally caught up with his quarry on the afternoon of December 10. More accurately, he had lost his way and was ambushed by them near Stormberg junction. Gatacre had served in India and the Sudan with some modest distinction but, like so many officers of his generation, modern ideas of intelligence and reconnaissance were regarded hardly at all. The Boer ambush was a complete surprise and just as complete a success; Gatacre was forced to withdraw leaving more than 500 of his men — nearly half his brigade — captive in Boer hands.

On the night of that same day, December 10,

Methuen launched his next attack. Between him and Kimberley there lay only one marked physical feature, a low ridge at Magersfontein. It was obvious that the ridge would form the main Boer line of defence and Methuen's strategy involved nothing more elaborate than a night approach and an attack at dawn, all of which was just as obvious to Boer general Cronje, now with his own reinforcements. Most of Cronje's 8,000 men were well dug in along the forward slopes of the ridge right down to the plain, and there were pom-poms and Maxim machine-guns just below the crest. His field-guns were on the reverse slope with observers passing back fall-of-shot signals, and below and behind them were the few sick and wounded, the horse-holders and some late-comers, to serve, just in case, as reserves.

Major-General Andrew Wauchope's Highland Brigade was given the honour of leading the advance, and they began to move up to their start line at midnight. It was pitch-black and drizzling and the early stage of the advance was made almost in lockstep so that no one would get lost. It took the Highlanders four hours to reach the last of the level ground before the rise of the Magersfontein Ridge. At the thin barrier of wire there, they began to spread out into a more open order for the attack, the four regiments in that brigade making a considerable noise as they moved across the rocky scrubland. Even the whispered orders of a hundred officers were a clear enough indication to the hidden Boers. Before the Scots had a chance to spread out, the waiting rifles, again at or near ground level, crashed out in a series of volleys which bit and ripped into the kilted ranks. Wauchope was among the first killed, and he was joined by many of his men.

As daylight came and then the hot lift of the sun, Methuen tried to relieve the situation, sending the Guards Brigade forward on the right and attempting to rally the shattered Highlanders. The Australian horsemen, held wide on a flank, could only watch, and what they saw was the first occasion in modern history on which Scots troops ran from the enemy. Neither those terrified soldiers nor the onlooking Australians saw that enemy, only the fatal effects of his gunfire.

Concealed from British infantry, Boer fighters lie in a long rifle-pit, scouring the veldt, with Mausers at the ready.

Methuen had lost a third of his strength. The Black Watch, the Seaforth Highlanders, the Argylls and the Highland Light Infantry were first-class regiments, but that brigade no longer had an effective fighting life. Methuen called off the assault on December 11. Beyond Magersfontein, Kimberley was still tightly locked in by Boer besiegers.

Four days later General Sir Redvers Buller, Commander-in-Chief in South Africa, went to the relief of Ladysmith on the eastern front in

In a traditional frontal assault, British troops clamber up a kopje, littered with their dead. Advancing upright, head unbowed, the British soldier presented an easy target to the Boer rifleman.

Natal. He led his five brigades and 44 guns toward the Tugela River, which looped across the veldt below a rocky ridge and with the village of Colenso in the curl of another loop on the right. To the right again was Hlangwane Hill, a Boer artillery position, well defended. Buller had advised the British Government of his intentions: "I feel I cannot force the Boer defences between here and Ladysmith and must turn them. To do this I have to march 50 miles."

That march was well under way when Buller changed his mind and told his staff that the column would cross the Tugela River at Colenso. He got a signal through to General Sir George White in Ladysmith telling him that he was on the way and would attack on December 17, and that White should attack his besiegers at the same time. Then, unaccountably, Buller ordered an attack at dawn on the next day, December 16, and did not advise White of that 24-hour timetable change.

Again, the few Australians attached to South African units among Buller's 15,000 men could do nothing but watch a scene of simple butchery. The Boer commander this time was the darkly handsome Louis Botha, a man who had opposed the war in parliament but who, once it began, gave himself to it wholeheartedly. At

Colenso he followed De la Rey's plan of concealment, pre-set ranges and patience.

Buller sent the Irish Brigade in on the left and Major-General Fitzroy Hart took them forward in parade-ground style, four regiments from Ireland marching in the close order of quarter-column, shoulder to shoulder. They followed a local guide into the loop of the river and found themselves in a bath of blood. The guide disappeared and from three sides the Boers in their rifle-pits opened fire. The Irish regiments went down like cut wheat. Those who could raised a screaming yell and charged into the water, but it was three metres deep with barbed wire below the surface. The survivors, dragging their wounded, backed out of that awful trap.

On the right, Major-General Henry Hildyard's 2nd Brigade had been put in to cross a wagon brigade over the river and take the village of Colenso itself. But Botha's guns were on the heights above and to the right of Colenso, and the British advance crumbled under the weight of artillery fire and the scything of musketry. Below Hlangwane Hill, from which the Boer field gunners had a clear line of fire, Lord Dundonald's cavalry, including the Australian Lancers, stood un-reinforced.

In the centre, Colonel C. J. Long, who had been ordered to support General Hildyard with his artillery, galloped his two field batteries much too far forward. Well back and away from Boer rifle fire, the guns of the Naval Brigade's battery did good work, engaging the Boer guns at a distance. Long's batteries were one-and-a-half kilometres ahead of their own line and only 500 metres from the enemy and, while the gunners served their guns magnificently their ammunition was soon exhausted and they had taken many casualties. Buller, arriving in that sector in a wild fluster, called for volunteers to save the guns and seven men ran immediately into the continuous shredding machine of rifle fire. Miraculously some survived and two guns were brought back. In that wild and gallant attempt to save what could be saved, and in yet another, just as reckless attempt, six Victoria Cross commendations were made, all posthumous, and 18 Distinguished Conduct Medals were awarded.

Buller pulled away, called back his command and marched it 11 kilometres to the rear to Frere, where he settled into a comfortable freshwater camp. He sent a signal to General White advising him to surrender Ladysmith. White, fortunately, chose to ignore the advice.

Buller had faced, at the most, 6,000 Boers under Louis Botha at Colenso. The British general had many more than twice that many in numbers and professional military skills abounded in his command, yet, in his haphazard and inept assault he had lost 11 of his 44 guns and 1,127 of his 15,000 men, including 240 missing and thought to be captured. The Boers lost no more than 50 men.

Suddenly Buller became known not as Sir Redvers but as "Sir Reverse". He was still, oddly, popular with the troops, but no longer in favour with his political masters in London. They sent out a new Commander-in-Chief, Field Marshal Lord Roberts of Kandahar whose son, Lieutenant the Honourable Frederick Roberts, had been one of those who tried to save Colonel Long's guns. The young man had earned a recommendation for the Victoria Cross, but had died of his wounds. Roberts, known throughout the Army as "Bobs", was both efficient and popular, but he was almost 68 and just about to retire from his post as C-in-C Ireland. His son's death had come as a great shock but it acted as a spur, too, and he accepted the new task grimly determined to set things right in South Africa.

There was a lot to do. Kimberley, Mafeking and Ladysmith were still under siege. The battles of Stormberg, Magersfontein and Colenso had been fought and lost between December 10 and December 17. The pride of British arms had been dragged in the dust of the veldt by Boer farmers, who were no longer thought of simply as "native rebels". Those disastrous days became known as "Black Week", and indeed, it had been just that.

LIFE ON THE VELDT

Near Mafeking, Australians in Colonel Plumer's relief force settle into their makeshift camp of thatched "humpies" and army-blanket tents.

"Every bushman is worth three soldiers because they can take care of themselves besides fighting."

A NSW Imperial Bushman enjoys a rest in his palatial shelter. Apart from his own blanket, he has scavenged materials like corrugated iron, stones and piled earth to make his camp a home away from home.

ANOTHER OUTBACK

As the war in South Africa progressed, British commanders realised that the ability to shoot and ride was essential to fighting the Boers on their own terms. Colonial soldiers had shown their Imperial officers in many actions that such skills were their bread and butter, making an impact on the fighting that far exceeded their numbers. The Australians substituted stealth and surprise for the British formula of massed infantry assaults and earned great respect from their ally and enemy.

Australian bushmen were hardened to the tough life in their own outback, and conditions on the veldt often reminded them of home. Corporal Gilfillan of the NSW Mounted Rifles described his first night in camp: "There are 10,000 troops here under canvas and we are camped in the middle of a great plain with not a tree in sight...nothing but a vast dried up land." Corporal J.H.M. Abbott of the Light Horse waxed lyrical about the veldt with its "Clear sunlight making lakes and lagoons before you, clearer and more distinct even than the mirage of our Western plains."

The bushmen could easily get about the seemingly featureless plains by day and night. They could kill and butcher their own meat, bake a damper in what coals could be had in timberless country and boil a billy on a very small fire. They swiped the odd duck, turkey or pig from an abandoned Boer farm, despite threatened punishment for looting. Like the Boer farmer-hunters, they lived off the land. As was their habit back home, these men had a strong partnership with their horses and were both conscientious and expert in their care. Able to keep long hours in the saddle, sleep rough, improvise shelter in the outdoors and endure extremes of climate, the bushmen formed the backbone of an effective fighting force which was strong and versatile enough to withstand the rigours of the South African campaign, and able to turn the tide against the Boer, beating him at his own artful game.

A sight familiar to soldiers from the Australian outback: a "dust-devil" whirls angrily among flimsy bell tents, choking and blinding man and horse alike. Dust storms were a regular scourge of camp life in South Africa.

Australian artillerymen tend to their personal mounts and the battery's gun-horses. Unacclimatised, underfed and overworked, horses suffered terribly in South Africa, but the Australians earned a reputation for putting their horses' well-being before their own.

All smiles, British and Australian soldiers receive their Christmas box of chocolates, a gift from Queen Victoria to her troops in Africa. The box often remained unopened, a souvenir for the folks back home.

An Australian rifleman contemplates a more extravagant meal than his issue of bully beef and biscuit. Despite stern and prompt punishment for looting, British and Australian troops poached pigs and fowl from Boer farmyards.

A NSW Bushman attracts the attention of a native South African family. Australians had a good rapport with native scouts.

Under the Union Jack, Australians sing hymns for victory on the Sunday church parade at Bulawayo.

Queensland "postmen" pick up the mail for delivery on horseback to forward camps. A well-regulated postal system by horse and mule-cart helped the flow of correspondence between home and the battlefield.

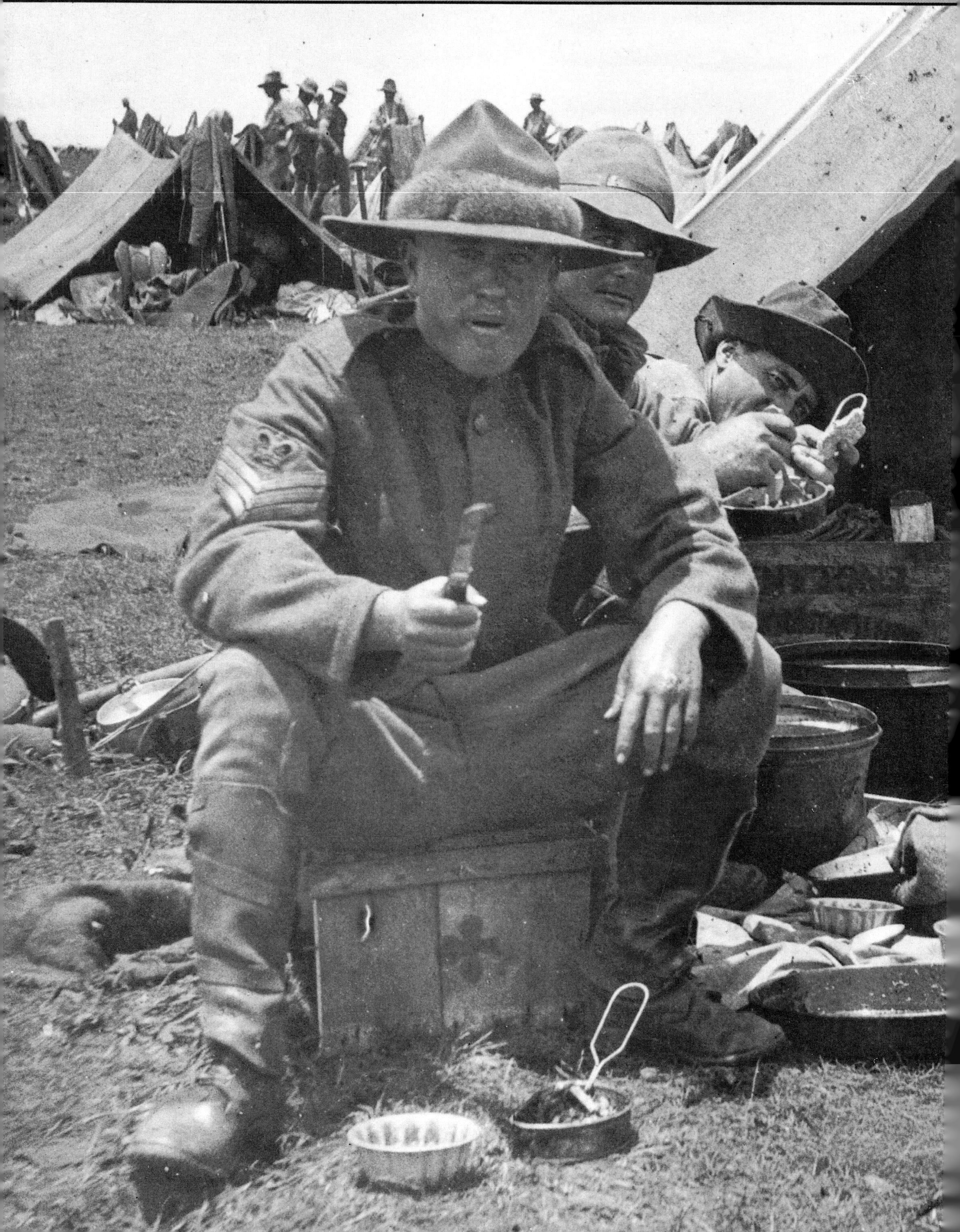

Troopers seek an uninterrupted lunch outside their simple tent. Make-do seating and utensils were part of everyday camp life.

5

ROBERTS TAKES THE REINS

As a new commander set things right for the Imperial army, Australian troops matched the Boers with bush skills and unyielding bravery. The fighting went Britain's way, but it was war as it had never been before.

There were enough men locked up in the three sieges to form a full division, and that fact, along with Black Week, had made it plain that it was going to take some real strength to put the Boers down. Roberts, still grieving for his dead son, plunged at once into a massive reorganisation and reinforcement of his forces. In Britain, the militia, the part-timers, were brought into a full-time active state, releasing the regular regiments engaged on home service for duty at the Cape. Many of the yeomanry and volunteer units whose charter called only for home service at once offered themselves for overseas postings, and, in the tradition of an earlier time, there were even some small, virtually private, units raised. Lord Loch, for instance, raised Loch's Horse in which one of his troop commanders was a retired Royal Navy Admiral. There were also many hundreds of willing volunteers in Cape Colony and Natal, local-born, some of them Boers who believed in the British cause. And there were the troops who had come enthusiastically to the Colours in Canada, New Zealand and Australia.

Roberts came ashore on the last day of December 1899. The next day Australian troops were in the thick of the action. At Sunnyside

Round-crowned felt hat, worn by many armies. This was later modified by Baden-Powell to become the well-known scouts hat.

Kopje, part of a group of low hills in the Vaal River plains west of Kimberley, Queensland Mounted Infantry with a support group of Canadians and local mounted infantry attacked a Boer position, but not in the British style. In thin, early-morning rain the little command, under Colonel T.D. Pilcher, dismounted and began carefully working up the east side of the kopje, drawing fire and returning it to keep the Boers' heads down. Pilcher also sent out a couple of four-man flank patrols so that his advance would not be caught in a crossfire. One of the patrols sprang just such a Boer trap, and a brisk fire-fight followed with casualties on both sides.

In the meantime, the two-company advance up the east side of the kopje slowly pushed the Boers back. By early afternoon one company had worked around the bulk of the rise on the western side. Colonel Pilcher signalled, and led both companies in a direct assault, catching the Boers front and rear; they surrendered and 40 prisoners were taken, together with a considerable quantity of arms and supplies in wagons. The Boers lost 30 men, killed and wounded; the Australians, two killed and two wounded.

It was the first success since Black Week, an excellent start to the new year, and it served notice to the Boers that here was a different kind of adversary, one needing to be treated with more respect than they had so far shown the British.

It was not that the bush skills and fighting qualities of the Australians always brought victory. A small patrol of NSW Lancers and Australian Horse, also a NSW unit, was ambushed near a farm at Slingersfontein, a hundred Boers suddenly riding hard at them, firing as they came. There was a shooting-match at the gallop and the Australians suffered badly; they lost 13 of the 24 men sent on that patrol.

It was part of the two-way learning process which went on while Roberts was reorganising. The war correspondent, A.G. Hales, reported a conversation with a wounded Boer prisoner in Bloemfontein Hospital. He had been one of 400 in a Boer commando near Slingersfontein, an irregular mounted force which attacked a small rise where 20 West Australian Mounted Infantry were positioned. Those men from the West staged a quite extraordinary defence, shielding themselves in the rock-strewn scrub, carefully picking their targets, shooting with great skill and repelling attack after attack with no loss to themselves till the Boers withdrew. Hales reported the wounded Boer survivor's comment: "There were 400 of us, all picked men. We dashed over the gully and charged up the kopje where those 20 men were waiting for us. But we did not know the Australians then. We know them now."

Roberts had wasted no time. He had brought with him as his chief of staff General Lord Kitchener, at the time still a major-general and famous for his campaign to reconquer the Sudan in 1896-1898, which culminated in victory at Omdurman outside Khartoum. Between them, the two men made swift and dramatic changes.

Buller was still in the field in Natal and, despite his marked lack of success, his command was the only one left untouched. But, he was given strict and constrictive orders to stand fast, to make no moves until he was told. At the Cape, Roberts determined to put as many of his troops as possible on horseback. The clear and punishing example of the Boer fighting style, plus the fact that the Australian mounted infantry was working successfully because it operated so much like the Boers, convinced him that the army had to be more mobile.

Mounted infantry was a dire need, and Roberts was not prepared to wait for men to be trained to ride elegantly enough to suit a cavalry horse-master. He wanted them mounted to move them, not to parade them. It became a matter of reshaping units so that anyone in an infantry regiment who could ride was put into a mounted infantry company; if there were not enough men in the regiment to form such a company, the riders were simply transferred into a new unit.

Among the newly arrived colonials there was no shortage of riders, only of military skills. But, one way and another, two new brigades of

A model of British orderliness, the camp at Slingersfontein is guarded by observation posts on high ground. In January 1900 a small Australian patrol was ambushed in this area and badly mauled.

mounted infantry were formed, and then there was only a shortage of horses. Kitchener overcame that by refusing to allow any transport to be horse-drawn; supply wagons had to hand over their teams and use oxen or mules instead. It was a temporary measure, but it served Roberts' first purpose, which was to get at the Boer and beat him. He planned to have Buller relieve Ladysmith while he concentrated a major force at the Modder River for a thrust through Bloemfontein to Pretoria, relieving Kimberley on the way.

Major-General John French, a lifetime cavalryman, was given a double brigade with which, initially, to keep the Boer horsemen, led by De la Rey and the Free State's Christiaan de Wet, busy enough so that the build-up at the Modder should not be disturbed. French's command included the NSW Lancers, the Queensland and the NSW Mounted Infantry, and two troops of the 1st Australian Horse, their Emu plumes waving alongside the helmets of historic British regiments like the Inniskilling Dragoons and the Scots Greys. The plan moved well and fast, except for Buller's part of it.

Though he had been ordered to make no moves, Buller disobeyed by taking his men into two disastrous battles. Fortunately for the Australians, none of their number were attached to his command. Buller took his British troops to attack the Boers in Natal and sent them across the Tugela River in a night attack to occupy the heights on the north bank. At first it seemed to be very successful, but then came the awakening. In the first light of day on January 23, 1900, the troops found themselves at the crest of a hill called Spion Kop, 500 metres high and with a flat top onto which the 2,000 of them were packed with little room or cover. It was surrounded by higher hills, all held by Boers. Worse, in the darkness they had not known that there were still many Boer marksmen on Spion Kop itself.

The fighting, first at artillery and rifle range, then hand-to-hand, went on through the length of a foully hot day and into the first fall of night. There were urgent calls for assistance, one from

121

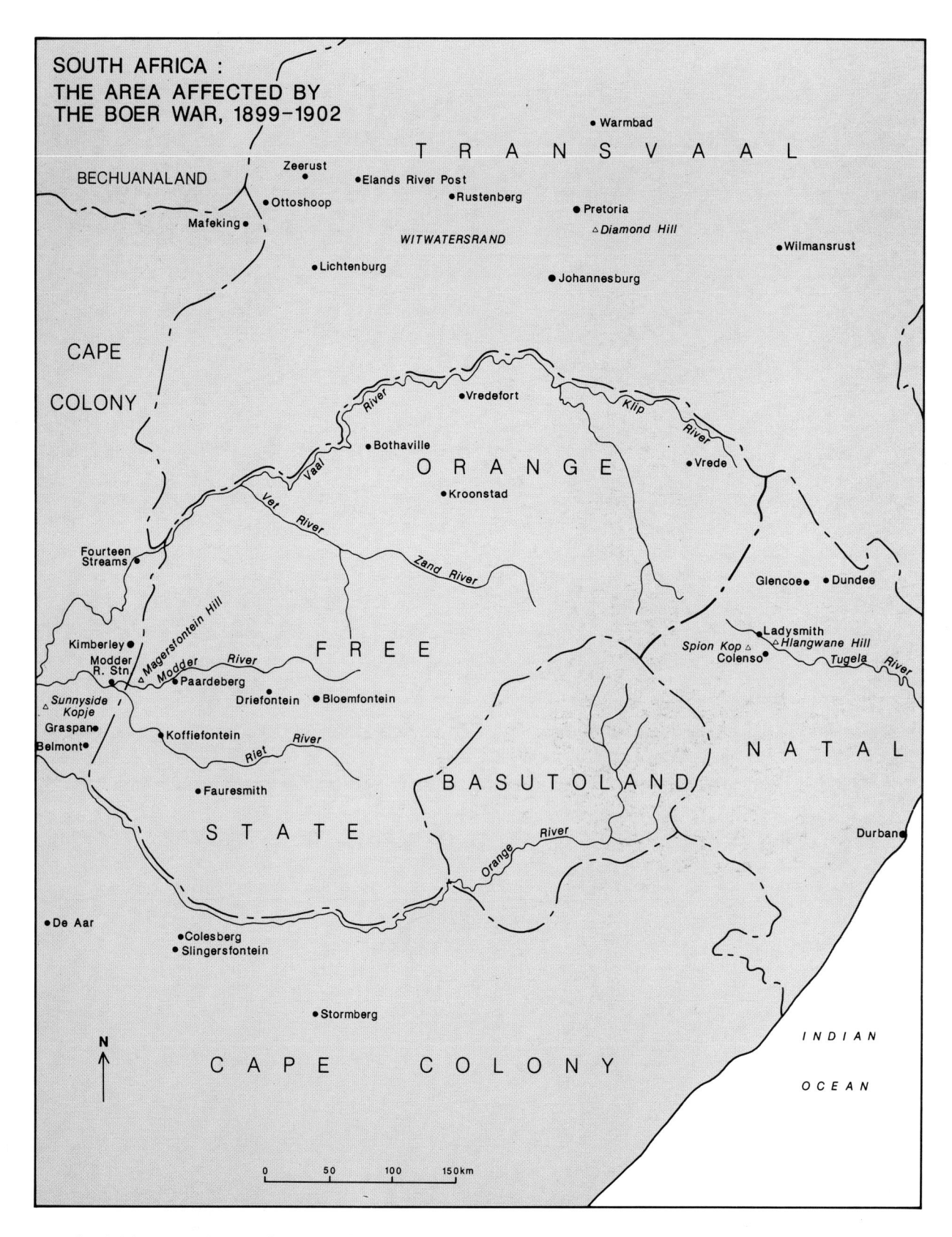

South Africa was split apart from 1899 after Boer forces besieged the three towns of Mafeking, Ladysmith, and Kimberley. Australian troops then joined Imperial forces in pursuit of rebel Boers across the country.

war correspondent Winston Churchill, who climbed the Kop to see for himself what was happening, but they went unheeded. That night those British troops still capable of movement retreated, leaving behind 1,200 men. It was the worst single defeat by a British army since the Crimea.

The Boers took full advantage of their victory. The photographs they took of the British dead were published world-wide and brought a howl of outrage in Britain. And still Buller plunged on. Two weeks later, on February 5, he attacked again, further west at Vaal Kranz and after six days of indecisive, inconclusive and expensive manoeuvring he again withdrew. His forces had managed to kill 42 Boers and wound another 50. He had lost another 408 dead, 1,390 wounded and 311 missing, probably captured.

In the meantime, while Buller blundered tragically about in Natal, Roberts had gone on the offensive in a very different fashion. He and General Kitchener — the troops called them "Bobs" and "K" — had put together a massive army to go against the Boers and they had done it in a remarkably short time. There were four infantry divisions, each of them with two four-battalion brigades and three batteries of field guns. There were the three brigades of a cavalry division, two brigades of first-line mounted infantry and seven horse batteries. Then came a second echelon which included not only the corps and service troops but a floating reserve of second-line mounted infantry and heavy artillery and howitzers. There were close to 30,000 infantry, 7,500 horsemen and 120 guns and, apart from the British regulars and London's City Imperial Volunteers, the first British volunteers ever to serve abroad, there were Australians, New Zealanders, Canadians and South Africans, on foot and in the saddle.

On February 11, 1900, Roberts launched this mass at the Boers. His plan was a diversionary one and involved sending Lord Methuen's 1st Division along the railway line to Kimberley, advancing them on a fairly broad front across the line to make General Piet Cronje think that it was the main assault and to convince him to hold his forces at Magersfontein. Cronje took that tempting bait, and by the time he realised he was wrong, he was too late.

Major-General John French's cavalry division, consisting of British and Australian horsemen, was the glittering point of Roberts' spearhead. It was sent wide, out to the east of Magersfontein in a great flanking arc, while the three other divisions of infantry and mounted infantry were to follow the cavalry hoofprints. The order was to relieve Kimberley at all costs.

There were costs, inevitably, for French drove his division hard. Arthur Conan Doyle, later famed for his Sherlock Holmes mysteries, served as a medical officer in one of the follow-up divisions; he wrote that French may have been a great cavalry commander, but he was a very bad horse-master.

It was high summer in the Orange Free State and that day, February 11, was to be one of the season's hottest. On that savagely speedy march under a hot-bronze sun, gun-horses collapsed and died in their traces, cavalrymen dismounted and trotted and walked alongside their hang-head horses and the back-trail was littered with dead, dying and distressed mounts — and men. One of French's brigades was largely made up of reservists who, five weeks earlier had been in the depths of a British winter; in that brigade, almost half the men collapsed from sunstroke, dehydration or heat exhaustion. It was a 40-kilometre march with no stopping for food or water, not for man or beast, and it took French's division slashing across the Reit River and on to the shallows at Klip Drift, on the Modder River. Twenty-one men died on that march, but the Boers, surprised, shocked and out-manoeuvred, pulled away leaving their supply wagons behind and sending messengers whipping their horses towards Cronje.

For a day there was some rest. The Modder gave them water, the Boer supplies gave them some extra flour and dried meat, and the follow-up divisions had time to join them. But French's patrols reported that Cronje, realising at last that he had been wrongfooted, was slipping men and guns down to block any further advance.

Lord Kitchener had visions of victory. He was as ruthless with his own troops as with the enemy.

Methuen's division was now astride the railway line and a strong threat which could not be ignored, but French's attack was suddenly the sword at the Boer throat and had to be dealt with. In the day it took the other divisions to catch up to French and for exhausted horses and men to rest, Cronje moved 1,000 of his men and a number of guns into the one position which effectively blocked the way to Kimberley, a line of low hills and a long, curving ridge, separated by a narrow nek. Through it, a pass led to the besieged town. The alternative was a long flank march under Boer fire all the way, and French was not prepared to make that move.

He gathered his division, British cavalry, Australian lancers and mounted infantry, and took them through that nek under the guns and rifles of the Boers waiting there. It was a classic cavalry charge, even if the mounted infantry had no chance to do more than ride hard and fire from the hip; for the Lancers, Hussars and Dragoons, British, Australian and South African, it was a case of lance-points down in the thrust and sabres out and swinging. French took them through at the full gallop, so fast that the Boer gunners could not alter range in time and their riflemen were unsighted by the combination of speed and the dust the charge raised.

Behind the charge, the following divisions moved in and through. And the gunfire lessened as, again, the Boers pulled out. As they moved back into the ring around Kimberley, an air of panic started to build and the besiegers began to limber up their guns and load their wagons, the solid ring thinning as the Boers slipped away.

French's men rested briefly on the far side of the nek. Patrols went out wide, water-bottles were tipped into plumed hats as NSW Lancers gave their horses a quick drink. Then the divisions formed up into column of route, cavalry leading, mounted infantry on the flanks and wheeling about to cover the rear.

In the late afternoon, the watchers in Kimberley saw a great pall of dust moving towards them across the veldt. There were fears that this was Cronje's army, massed finally to break their obstinate resistance to the siege, but the crashing gunfire which had for so long ripped into the town, had slackened and died. People began to come out of their shelters and out of the mine shafts where the shells of the huge Creusot-made "Long Tom" siege-guns could not reach them. They began to see lance pennons in the dust cloud and to recognise the solar helmets, the khaki, and the wide-brimmed bush hats, and a great shout went up. A patrol of Australian Horse wheeled into Kimberley's main street and cleared a path for French to lead his men in among the cheering, weeping people.

For 124 days there had been a ring of steel around that diamond town. No fewer than 1,500 of its inhabitants, white and native, had died from wounds or illness, but they had held together, helped by the example of Cecil Rhodes who had once wielded, then yielded, great power and who, during the siege, was a fellow citizen and a hard-working organiser. For that time, at least, it was perhaps possible for them to forget that he was as responsible as anyone for the war which had brought them under the Boer gun.

In a costly blunder, General Buller sends his troops across the Tugela River intending to capture the hills beyond in a daring night raid. The following day, 2,000 men found themselves trapped on Spion Kop, surrounded by Boers on higher ground.

Hundreds of British dead are heaped ignominiously in a shallow trench after their spirited but doomed resistance on Spion Kop. This, and other grisly photographs, were taken by the victorious Boers, who arranged their publication to break Britain's nerve.

The siege of Kimberley was lifted on February 15, 1900. The next day Roberts ordered French to mount and ride again. Piet Cronje, tough, wily and determined, was still at large and the word was that he was moving east with a long train of wagons and cape carts and a considerable force. Roberts wanted him stopped and caught — or killed.

French, always anxious to close with the enemy, had a sizeable problem which was to bedevil the army time and again. He was short of horses. The hard ride up, and the charge, had left his horse-lines full of lame, blown and exhausted mounts; he found that he could put no more than 2,000 of his men in the saddle, less than half his riders. But it did not stop him.

He took the 2,000 out on a black midnight, riding south-east at a good clip, knowing that Cronje's column was limited by the slow pace of its ox-drawn wagons. The Boers were making for Bloemfontein, and the track would take them via Paardeberg, the last shallow crossing-place on the Modder River. Scouts reported the line of Cronje's march to French, and the general and his men, riding whip and spur for the last few kilometres, headed the Boers off, holding them away from the Paardeberg crossing.

Then, behind them, came Roberts' infantry and the rest of the mounted infantry and the guns, the two jaws of the pincer closing. Cronje's Boers dug in, leaving Christiaan de Wet's light and mobile irregular troops, his commando, who had come out of their own hiding place 50 kilometres to the south to rescue

Lord Frederick Sleigh Roberts, the British commander, and his Indian aide.

THE GREAT STRATEGIST

Frederick Sleigh Roberts was born in Cawnpore, India in 1832 and sent to England for his schooling. He was commissioned into the Bengal Army in 1851. Six years later, as a twenty-five-year-old lieutenant, he earned the Victoria Cross during the Indian Mutiny. By 1880 he held the brevet-rank of major-general and commanded a field force in Afghanistan, where he led ten thousand men on an epic march to relieve the garrison of Kandahar. His excellent tactics resolved the long-running Afghan War.

In 1895 he was appointed as Commander-in-Chief Ireland and in 1900, as a 67-year-old field-marshal, called to replace Buller. Roberts brought dispassionate planning and order to the campaign in South Africa; he recognised the need for more mobility in his forces and pushed for the formation of more Yeomanry and for more colonial mounted soldiers. He relinquished his command to Kitchener in 1901 and returned to England where he was appointed Commander-in-Chief of the army and created Earl Roberts of Kandahar, but till his death in 1914, he was known affectionately to his Indian troops as ''Bobs Bahadur'' and to British soldiers simply as ''Bobs''.

Cronje's men, to skirmish as best they could around the now encircling British forces.

The British Commander-in-Chief was unwell at this time; Roberts had an uncomfortable summer cold, he was nearing 70, the weather had been very hot and sultry, and conditions in the field were not the easiest. He turned over command to Kitchener for the time being. That was on February 18, and Kitchener at once launched a curiously uncoordinated attack, more a series of probes, put in piecemeal against Cronje's *laager*, his fortified camp of wagons and quickly dug trenches. For two days, Kitchener urged his troops on, riding among them to push them forward and, it appeared, not caring about the heavy casualties which resulted. At one stage, he ordered the entire mounted brigade to ride on the trenches.

Their colonel, reluctant but unable to refuse the direct order, took only a small group of his men, less than a squadron, and put them to the charge, himself at their head. He was killed instantly and the survivors of the futile attempt wheeled back into their own lines.

During two days under Kitchener, the losses were 320 dead and 942 wounded. Late on February 27, Roberts took over again, still unwell but not at all pleased by the casualty reports. He made sure the encirclement of the Boers was complete, put out mounted infantry to handle de Wet's skirmishers and began a systematic bombardment of Cronje's position while the army watched and waited.

For eight days the Boers held out, clinging bitterly to their positions, but taking heavy casualties, among them some of the women and children in Cronje's wagon-train. For much of that time there was torrential summer rain, and the roar and flash of the artillery were more than matched by night-long storms of thunder and lightning. The Modder River rose high above that last drift, the crossing which would have taken Cronje to Bloemfontein and safety.

The siege could not last. The combination of continuous artillery bombardment and a lack of food weakened the Boers to the point where Piet Cronje could not see them suffer more.

With the 4,000 fighting men under his hand he probably could have broken out of the trap at some point, but he refused and refused again to leave the women and children and the wounded to save himself. He surrendered on February 27, 1900, and was given breakfast at Roberts' own camp, but at a separate table from the C-in-C. It was 19 years to the day since the Boers had slaughtered and humiliated the British at Majuba Hill.

Yet the British revenge was not complete. In Natal there was still General "Sir Reverse" Buller, smarting under the nickname and anxious to wipe away the disasters of Colenso and Spion Kop and Vaal Kranz. While the artillery at Paardeberg was hammering Cronje's men, Buller attacked the Boers in a fully professional fashion, starting with the capture of Hlangwane Hill, where the Australian horsemen had fretted at their inaction during the battle for Colenso. That gave him command of the Tugela River, and he crossed it and advanced on the Boer lines at Pieter's Hill, determined to break through to Ladysmith.

The garrison there had held firm for 100 days under General Sir George White, the man who had once ignored Buller's advice to surrender. White's troops won a major fight in the first week of the new year when several thousand picked marksmen under the Boer Commandant Villiers tried to break the defence line but were forced back with 800 casualties. Since then they had been under almost continuous artillery bombardment, but now weak, many of them sick from the continual fighting and diminishing rations, they could sense the tide turn.

Buller used his troops like a spendthrift, throwing General Hart's Irish Brigade, which had already suffered so badly at Colenso, directly at the Boers. They lost almost half their number without taking the position. It was not until Buller pushed the Natal Carbineers and the Imperial Light Horse forward into the Boer left wing, reinforcing each successful thrust immediately, that the line was broken. He had lost 1,896 men, killed and wounded.

He marched in to relieve Ladysmith on February 28, the day after the anniversary of Majuba Hill, and he and his men were shocked at the physical state of the garrison. Of the original force of 14,000, only 2,000 were fit enough to join in the pursuit of Louis Botha's retreating Boers. White himself was ill and had to be invalided home. Buller followed him two months later, still, despite his losses, held high in the affection of his troops for whose welfare he cared greatly — except, it seemed, in battle.

Kimberley and Ladysmith were again in British hands, but Christiaan de Wet was still out there on the veldt, his cavalry command a rallying point for the Boers. The heavy rain had greened the land and there was plenty of food for de Wet's horses. The local people provided food and he was well enough stocked with weapons and ammunition, a good deal of it taken from the British army. He made a stand at Dreifontein Kopjes — the Hills of the Three Springs — and was found and attacked there on March 10, as Roberts led his army towards Bloemfontéin.

Banjo Paterson, riding with French's cavalry column, reported in the *Sydney Morning Herald* how the 1st Australian Horse was sent to assault the position dismounted and how they moved up through the long grass towards de Wet's waiting rifles: "For a great part of their advance they were hidden from the Boers by the swell of the hill above them. But all of a sudden they came in sight of the Boers. The way they dropped down and melted into the grass was astonishing, as at one moment the hillside was alive with men; at the next moment the khaki uniforms had blended with the brown grass, and there wasn't a man to be seen. But the sharp cracking of the rifles told that they were busily at work."

Roberts' artillery fired over the Australians' heads and the Boers began to go for their horses and ride off at speed. The situation suddenly seemed to become an all-Australian one with the NSW and the Queensland Mounted Infantry knee to knee to take the enemy guns which were still firing. When the order for a general advance and a pursuit of the fleeing Boers came down, not one of the British cavalry regiments was capable of moving; their horses, they reported, were exhausted. Yet, despite the fact that it would soon enough be night, the NSW Lancers and the 1st Australian Horse set off on the chase at once. But de Wet's men had too much of a start and were lost in the dark.

It took almost a fortnight to reach Bloemfontein, capital of the Orange Free State. That substantial city lay in a nest of hills thick with Boer marksmen and with a number of machine-gun and pom-pom positions, all well dug in. The advance had to contend with more rain and the consequent mud, with low and poor rations and with constant fire. But Roberts was marching now with his whole army at hand and with reinforcements which had been brought forward. It was an irresistible move as the Boers could see well enough. And when French, in command of the vanguard, began a heavy bombardment over his cavalry's heads, the Boer wagons could be seen lurching and bumping away, de Wet's commando doing their best to screen them.

On March 13, 1900, Roberts and Kitchener rode into Bloemfontein at the head of a successful army. In less than 12 weeks in South Africa they had turned the war around.

Through to the end of March and through all of April, 1900, Roberts and his army rested at Bloemfontein. It was not a rest in the simple sense of the word, not just a relaxation and recuperation, although that formed some part of that six-week spell.

There was a severe epidemic of enteric fever which filled hospital beds and kept a quarter of the army out of any effective work at one time or another. The Army Medical Service benefitted greatly from the work of the first women to go to war for Britain since Florence Nightingale's time, among them the grey-cloaked sisters of the colonies. There were Australian fighting doctors there too, including a young lieutenant, Neville Howse, who galloped into intense Boer fire to rescue a wounded trumpeter and to treat his wounds. Howse won

An enormous hot-air reconnaissance balloon is used for judging the strength of General Cronje's forces at Magersfontein in preparation for Roberts' double-pronged advance on Kimberley. The British used military balloons for accurate sightings of artillery barrages.

a Victoria Cross for that gallant deed.

Roberts also was faced with the need to bring several thousand horses up to condition again, a task which could not be rushed. There was the sadder business of putting down horses too ill or too weak to be maintained, and then the awkward job of working-in the remounts, many of them very poor quality stock bought hurriedly in the Argentine and quite wild even before the long sea trip. This was an area in which Australian bushmen came to the fore, dazzling British troops with their mastery of horse-breaking techniques. Among them was the near-legendary Harry Morant, a bush-balladist and horseman known as "The Breaker".

For Roberts there was a further urgent need: to secure lines of communication southwards, down the railway line to the Cape. He needed replacements for his dead, wounded and sick and had asked for reinforcements too. And he needed a huge stockpile of supplies for the next phase of his plan. That was the taking of Pretoria, the clearing of the Transvaal and the defeat of the remaining Boer forces.

For no matter how successfully Roberts had advanced, no matter that he was consolidating a strong position and reinforcing it, there was always the knowledge that there were Boers in the field, out on the veldt, up in the mountains, fiercely independent and still hell-bent on beating the British. And chief among them was Christiaan de Wet who had developed into a past-master at the use and movement of light cavalry and mounted men in conjunction with fast-moving field-batteries. He was intent on giving Roberts' army as little rest as possible and constantly harassed and harried anything he could reach. The army nicknamed him the "Phantom of the Veldt", and at the end of March he achieved a notable victory.

At Sannah's Post, a new waterworks had been established to serve Bloemfontein, and camped there was a fair-sized British force under Colonel R.G. Broadwood. He had three squadrons of cavalry, two Royal Horse Artillery batteries and a large convoy with an infantry escort. De Wet led a couple of troops of heavy field-guns and 2,000 riflemen into position under cover of darkness and opened fire on the camp at first light. Broadwood ordered his force out of their exposed encampment and into the open country towards Bloemfontein, assuming

SISTERS OF WAR

Hundreds of Australian women, both professional and unqualified, offered to go as nurses with the first contingent to the Boer War, but their applications were, to begin with, turned down by Imperial authorities. A quota was, however, accepted for the second contingent which set sail in December 1899 with 14 nurses from NSW, 10 from Victoria and three from South Australia. A freelance nurse from NSW had already paid her own way over earlier in the war and other individuals followed her example so that, eventually, about 60 nurses from the colonies served in South Africa. These brave women nursed the sick and wounded in field hospitals, under canvas, and town hospitals, both army and civilian, in locations on and behind the battlefields in Natal, the Orange Free State, the Transvaal and Cape Colony.

Disease claimed more lives in the Boer War than did shot and shell. The appalling conditions under which the nurses worked — poor hygiene, overcrowding and chronic shortages of doctors, orderlies, bedding, dressings, food, water and medicine — were particularly acute in typhoid-ridden Bloemfontein where the NSW Army Corps took over the military barracks and converted them into a 150-bed hospital. As the typhoid epidemic raged, the sick were packed close on the floors with only a single blanket for each man to lie on. Sister Annie Matchett of NSW described the problems of daily life: "There is no gas or electric light in Bloemfontein. Candles are very scarce; wood and coal are scarce also. It is most difficult to get hot water at night. We all have spirit lamps but no methylated spirits is to be had in town. All the shops are empty. There are a great many deaths here. We counted 20 funerals in one day. They have no coffins, the dead are merely stitched up in a grey blanket and carried to the cemetery on stretchers".

With working days frequently reaching 15-hour, unrelieved stretches and often enduring frightful living conditions, some nurses succumbed to illness and death. Frances Emma Hines from Victoria died of pneumonia on August 7, 1900, and lies buried at Bulawayo under a marble memorial cross erected by the Victorian Bushmen and her colleagues.

For their stoicism and dedication in the face of disheartening odds and sordid circumstances, three Australian nursing sisters received the Royal Red Cross — Queen Victoria's award for women who nurse the sick and wounded in war. They were E. Nixon from NSW, M.S. Bidsmead from South Australia, and Superintendent M. Rawson from Victoria.

that the Boers would not venture that close to the city and the main army. It was not till he was out on the veldt that he found how wrong he was. The audacious de Wet had set an ambush there, in the open country, and forced Broadwood to stand and fight. It was a savage encounter and, although Broadwood managed to pull out and get back to Bloemfontein, he lost 19 of his officers and 136 men killed or wounded, 426 prisoners, seven of the RHA guns and the whole of his convoy. The Queensland Mounted Infantry rode out at the gallop to help and they lost two dead, two wounded and five captured. It was a harsh reminder to Roberts and all his army that there was still a war on.

Nonetheless, within and around Bloemfontein, the army gathered and repaired itself, taking on a slightly different organisational shape. Major-General Ian Hamilton was given command of a detached force, 16,000 strong, which included a new formation, sensibly grouping the increasingly useful mounted infantry into a single division. Major-General "Curly" Hutton was given one of the division's brigades. Aside from four battalions of Imperial troops, and some New Zealanders and Canadians, Hutton led the men he knew best, the NSW Mounted Infantry and their fellows from all the other Australian colonies.

By the end of April, Roberts was satisfied with the state of the army and, on May 3, 1900, its leading elements swung out of Bloemfontein in crisp autumn weather, out onto the veldt where the grass stood knee-high to the rested horses. There was a long way to go — 130 kilometres northwards to the Vaal River, heading ultimately towards Pretoria — and, even though conditions were good, it was to be no easy march.

Hamilton's division bore out wide to the east, about 70 kilometres from the huge spread of the main body. Winston Churchill, who had escaped from Boer captivity in Pretoria and was looking forward to going back there under different circumstances, rode with Hamilton's men and he later told something of that "jolly march" which lasted six weeks: "We lived on flocks of sheep which we drove with us, and chickens which we hunted round the walls of deserted farms. Nearly every day there was the patter of rifle-fire in front, on the flank, or more often at the heels of the rear-guard. Every few days, a score of our men cut off, ambushed or

Victorian Nursing Sister Janey Lempriere and her colleague at the General Field Hospital in Capetown. Compared with conditions in the besieged cities and near the battlefields, this hospital under canvas, with electricity and water supplied, was a haven for the sick and wounded.

With the railway link destroyed, a British column uses a pontoon bridge to cross the Orange River, March 1900.

entrapped, made us conscious of the great fighting qualities of these rifle-armed horsemen of the wilderness."

At one point Hamilton's division was swung across from the east to the west flank of the advance, for Roberts thought that was where the main Boer resistance would be. In fact, despite constant harassment, there was no real resistance to that rolling horde — 45,000 men, 11,000 horses, 120 guns and more than 2,500 wagons. On May 12, the rail junction at Kroonstad was taken, the halfway mark on Roberts' road. The mass of men pushed forward, a little slower as the land lifted beneath their feet, 1,500 metres and more above sea level, the air thinner, the horses beginning to blow a little.

Across in the east, in Natal, the last Boer resistance was swept away at Glencoe and Dundee, and on May 24, the Orange Free State was, yet again, annexed by Britain as a colony. That was just a week after a flying column of Hussars was sent by Roberts under Colonel Bryan Mahon to relieve Mafeking in conjunction with a column which galloped across the Rhodesian border, led by Colonel Plumer and with a number of Queenslanders in its ranks. The seven-month siege of Mafeking was lifted on May 17, 1900, the garrison celebrating with a modest ceremonial march-past of the relief column, at which Baden-Powell took the salute. Around him the township's shattered buildings were covered in bunting — the parade also celebrating the Queen's birthday.

Ahead of Roberts to the north, was the goldrich rise of Witwatersrand, the fabulous Rand; and then there was the prize of Johannesburg and the Transvaal and, north again, Pretoria. But between them and Roberts stood Louis Botha, full of fight, holding a line on the Klip River, south of Johannesburg, and determined to deny its crossings to the British. He and his men tried desperately hard, but they could not stand against the tide of men coming at them, Australians to the fore.

While the New South Welshmen in Roberts' spearhead drew Boer fire as a diversion, Queenslanders crossed at a ford and took and held some commanding hills. Western Australians found another ford and crossed there and held fast. The next day, General Ian Hamilton was able to bring his division up and put it across the river, under heavy fire, taking casualties but unstoppable by Botha's force. The first troops into Johannesburg were Australians, a troop of South Australian Mounted Infantry under Lieutenant Peter Rowell. It was May 31.

Two days later, the army was on the move again towards Pretoria, the seat of government and home of Paul Kruger. But Kruger had gone away nearly two weeks before, through Portuguese territory to Europe. The men who remained there were no less important figures: the President of the Orange Free State, Marthinus Steyn, Commando Commandant Martin Prinsloo, and the Phantom himself, Christiaan de Wet. Botha swung a strong rearguard in behind de Wet as he took Steyn out of the city. Roberts marched in on June 5 without resistance, and at once sent troops after the escapees who were away into the rough crags of mountain range that lay to the east of the city, the Boer rearguard covering their run.

New South Welshmen and Western Australians dismounted and, fighting hand-to-hand with bayonets, attacked the rearguard at Diamond Hill, capturing Botha's key positions and forcing his withdrawal. Other troops scrambled quickly for the passes through the range, but Commandant Prinsloo and his commando moved faster and held an open way for the President and the Phantom. On June 18, those two key figures slipped out of the British and Australian net and were gone.

In the bleak and wet dawn of the next day, the slow and awkward Boer supply wagons were halted and captured. Even without the encumbrance of the wagon train, and with all the countryman's skills at his command, Prinsloo was already effectively trapped. He broke his men off into groups as small as a dozen, but all around him troops suddenly appeared everywhere in the mountains. Prinsloo, seeing no way out, surrendered himself and almost 4,000 men by the end of the month.

It now seemed that Boer forces were on the decline. There had been reports that Boer fighters in the West Transvaal were handing in their rifles after Pretoria had been returned to British hands. But, by mid-1900, the region west of there to Mafeking was again alive with elusive commandos causing a constant menace to Roberts' supply lines.

Roberts ordered a small guard force to safeguard Elands River Post, where there was a supply dump with £100,000 worth of stores and ammunition; the post was near a shallow river

THE PHANTOM BOER

Christiaan de Wet was born into an established Boer family and he showed a bright intelligence from boyhood. Unlike the Boers of the veldt, de Wet was a city man, a successful and respected businessman, and his solid figure and calm, heavily bearded face gave little impression of his agile, ferocious and original mind. In the early part of 1900 he used a commando of 1,500 of his best men to skirt the edges of the British army's 30,000, ripping into stragglers and exposed flank units, savaging supply wagons, darting into unsuspecting patrols and then disappearing. He earned the nickname, "The Phantom of the Veldt". He continued his ferocious harassment of the British into the last days of the war. Kitchener swore to "bag" this "slippery customer", but he swore in vain.

It is sad — and seems not to fit the legend — that this dashing fighter should have ended his life so miserably. In 1914 he was one of the leaders of a rebellion against the Union of South Africa and its pro-British stance. The rising failed, de Wet was arrested, spent a year in prison and eventually died in 1922, a solitary and lonely man whose past glory was forgotten.

crossing 35 kilometres west of Pretoria, and it was considered vital that the ford be kept open for the passage of troops.

For the first time in the war Australian troops under no officers but their own, went into the field as a single unit, and even had others under command. Colonel Hore of the Queensland Mounted Infantry was the officer commanding and he had almost 150 of his troopers with him; there were 100 NSW Citizen Bushmen, 40 Victorian Bushmen, nine from Western Australia and two more from Tasmania. With them went 200 troopers of the Rhodesian Volunteers and a handful of Canadian and British horsemen. Other than their personal weapons they had an old muzzle-loading 7-pounder and two Maxim machine-guns.

A strong Boer commando struck at Colonel Hore's force as it made for Elands River and there was a brisk running fight as the Australians pulled into the post, to form a garrison of little more than 500. They began to dig in and fortify at once, using wagons, boxes, and bags of flour daubed in mud to cover their whiteness — anything which would offer some protection. The post was on a low, flat-topped hill looking out on open and rocky terrain; higher, more rugged hills rose to overlook the Australians' puny defence-ring and the Boers were quick to close around the post and begin sniping.

Before the net closed a message was got out when a young Englishwoman, a local farmer's wife, rode till she found an army detachment who passed her back to their headquarters. In the meantime the Australians, far from adopting a siege mentality, began to push fighting-patrols forward, probing at the Boer forces which were swelling day by day. On July 19, Colonel Hore sent out a full squadron of his Queenslanders to escort in to the post a supply column which had been following behind his troops and from its officers he learned that local intelligence placed De la Rey and a possible 2,000 to 3,000 Boers in the nearby hills. And they were moving down — with field-guns.

The first Boer artillery opened fire two days later, the barrage getting steadily heavier as more guns were brought to bear. It was estimated that there were more than a thousand shells of varying calibre fired into the perimeter on one day, but either the Boer gunners were ill-trained or the Australian defenders were too well dug in; casualties were very light although there was damage to the few buildings, among them one used, and marked, as a hospital.

The Australians countered the cannonading and the frighteningly accurate sniping of the Boers by making their moves at night. Carriers edged down to the river at night to fetch up water, and shattered defences were repaired at night. Most tellingly, the Australians went out in the darkness and slid unheard into the enemy lines, killing in silence so that a Boer often enough would wake in the false dawn to find the man next to him dead. Where a gun position could be reached, a fighting-patrol would move out behind the shield of night, creep close, make a sudden and deadly rush against the gun-crew and vanish into the darkness. These were tactics which surprised, worried and, in many cases, frightened the Boers; they did not, though, stop the gunfire and the sniping.

The promised relief column never arrived. It ran into a small Boer force with which it skirmished, then it retreated 20 kilometres and sent a message back to Lord Roberts saying that the Elands River defenders must have surrendered. Then the relievers withdrew. Colonel Baden-Powell, commanding at Mafeking, began to move to the relief but thought he heard all sounds of firing stop. He, too, assumed there had been a surrender and stayed put.

There had, indeed, been the chance to surrender. On August 8, De la Rey sent a flag-of-truce messenger to advise Colonel Hore of the retreat of the relief force, to let the defenders know that the whole area was in Boer hands, and to promise them the full honours of war if they would yield. They could march out with their weapons and he would guarantee safe conduct for them to the nearest British garrison. As an alternative he offered destruction by his artillery. The offer was politely refused and the crash of exploding shells began again.

FOR VALOUR

It is one of the least ornate and one of the most highly treasured awards in the world. Made from the bronze of cannon captured at Sevastopol during the Crimean War, the Victoria Cross has been awarded to 96 Australians — and there would have been six more except that no posthumous awards were made during the Boer War; in those six cases there was only an announcement in the *London Gazette* that had the man concerned lived he would have been recommended for the award.

Queen Victoria's warrant instituting the bronze cross named for her was issued in 1856 and said of the new decoration that Her Majesty was "desirous it should be highly prized and eagerly sought after by Officers and Men of Our Naval and Military Service." It was to be awarded "to those officers and men who have served Us in the presence of the enemy and shall then have performed some single act of valour or devotion to their country. Neither rank nor long service nor wounds nor any other circumstance or condition whatsoever save the merit of conspicuous bravery shall be held to establish a sufficient claim for the honour."

The Victoria Cross had been in existence for 44 years when it was awarded for the first time to an Australian soldier, and that first Australian recipient of the Victoria Cross was not formally an Australian at all. Neville Howse was born in Somerset, England, and migrated to Australia in 1899 where he set up his first practice as a newly qualified doctor. It was as a doctor, as a lieutenant in the New South Wales Medical Corps, that he sailed for South Africa in February 1900, almost a full year before the colonies had become the nation of Australia.

On July 24, 1900, he was serving with a mounted infantry brigade which was heavily engaged in a fight with General Christiaan de Wet's commando. As a line of horsemen charged towards the Boer position a young trumpeter fell wounded and Howse, seeing the lad fall, mounted and rode into very heavy fire to rescue him. His horse was shot from under him but he reached the trumpeter, dressed his wounds and carried him out of the line of fire and to safety.

Neville Howse VC in his World War I uniform.

The 37-year-old Lieutenant Howse was to live another 30, very eventful years, becoming Mayor of Orange, NSW, leaving that office to enlist in 1914 and going with the Naval and Military Expedition to seize German New Guinea. He landed at Gallipoli on the first day, became Surgeon-General and Director of Medical Services to the AIF, turned to politics after the war and was a member of the National Party and served in the Cabinet three times. In addition to his VC, Neville Howse was created a Knight Commander of the Bath, Knight Commander of St. Michael and St. George and a Knight of Grace of the Order of St. John of Jerusalem.

He was the most honoured of the Boer War VCs from Australia, but the others, like Howse, showed a follow-up pattern in their lives which seemed to indicate that they were not men for whom a single act of outstanding bravery was enough.

Lieutenant Frederick Bell of the 6th Mounted Infantry, Trooper John Bisdee of the Tasmanian Imperial Bushmen, Lieutenant Leslie Maygar of the Victorian Mounted Rifles, Sergeant James Rogers of the South African Constabulary and Lieutenant Guy Wylly, another Tasmanian Bushman, all had similar experiences on the way to the Victoria Cross. Each of them rode into heavy enemy fire to go to the rescue of comrades; each of them either lost his horse to that gunfire or took a wounded man's horse; each of them performed with cold courage in the face of great odds and each of them lived to be successful, either as a soldier or in public service.

Leslie Maygar was the shortest-lived. He volunteered in 1914 and served on Gallipoli, rose to command the 8th Light Horse and, as a lieutenant-colonel, was in temporary command of the 3rd Light Horse Brigade. He died of wounds in 1917, at Beersheba.

Fred Bell joined the British Colonial Service in Somaliland and became a noted lion-hunter. He went to war again in 1914 with the Royal Irish Dragoon Guards and by 1918 was a lieutenant-colonel commanding an embarkation camp. He went back to Africa, again in the Colonial Service, until his retirement. He was 79 when he died in Bristol in 1954.

John Bisdee stayed in the army and in 1915 was given command of the 12th Light Horse as a major, was wounded in the leg, served as an assistant provost marshal in Egypt and then, after a spell back with his own Light Horse regiment, was promoted to lieutenant-colonel and was second-in-command of the Anzac Provost Corps. His VC was later followed by an OBE and he retired from military life to farm in Tasmania until his death in 1930.

James Rogers was commissioned as lieutenant in 1902 and, like the others, fought again a few years later. He was at Gallipoli, was wounded there and then, like Bisdee, served in the Anzac Provost Corps until he was invalided from the service in 1916 with the honorary rank of captain. He stayed with the reserve of officers until 1922 and then ran a successful grazing property until his death in 1961, aged 86.

Guy Wylly transferred to the Indian Army in 1902 and in 1909 became aide-de-camp to Lord Kitchener. The Great War saw him serving as a staff captain and then brigade major with the Indian Cavalry Division in France. He was badly wounded in the face but recovered and was posted as General Staff officer with Australian troops from mid-1916. He was entered into the Distinguished Service Order in 1918 and went back to the Indian Army on the North-West Frontier until his retirement from active service as an honorary colonel in 1933. He was created Companion of the Order of the Bath and went to live in Britain where he died, aged 82, in 1962.

BATTLE HIGHLIGHTS OF THE BOER WAR

The main ebb and flow of the Boer War clouded the individual contribution of Australian troops in South Africa. As Boer forces at first bested the Imperial army, then as British and colonial forces hit back to beat the Boers into submission, Australians were involved in skirmishes at the main front and away from it, matching Boer commandos in isolated parts of the country. Australians served alongside units from Britain and other colonies in most of their actions, and accounts of major battles often failed to distinguish the nationality of Imperial soldiers involved. Wherever they served, Australian soliders played a significant part in the overall Imperial victory.

More than 16,000 Australian volunteers fought in South Africa, in 57 contingents: 15 from NSW, nine each from Queensland, South Australia, and Western Australia, eight from Victoria and seven from Tasmania. They took with them more than 16,000 horses and 220 guns and wagons. Most of them were mounted infantry suited to the terrain and the Boer style of warfare, a fact borne out by the Australians' light casualties: 1,400 all up, including wounded, with 251 killed in action and 257 dying from disease.

Of the hundreds of incidents involving Australian soliders, a chronology of the highlights clearly shows the colonials were the kind of fighters that could turn the tide of the war.

DATE	UNIT	EVENT
1899		
Oct. 12	—	Outbreak of war
Nov. 23	NSW L	at Battle of Belmont Hill
Nov. 25	NSW L	at Graspan. Hold hill
Nov. 28	NSW L	at Battle of Modder River
Dec. 6	VMR, SA, WA, TAS Infantry	form Australian Regiment
Dec. 8	NSW L	at capture of Arundel
Dec. 10	—	British reverse, Stormberg
Dec. 11	NSW L	British reverse, Magersfontein
Dec. 15	—	British reverse, Colenso
Dec. 17	—	Lord Roberts appointed CinC
Dec. 30	NSW MR	proceed to Prieska
1900		
Jan. 1	1 QMI	in successful attack at Sunnyside
Jan. 16	NSW L, NSW MR	skirmish at Slingersfontein
Feb. 9	Aust. Regt.	Heavily engaged at Jasfontein, Slingersfontein
Feb. 12	1 VMR	in serious action, Pink Hill
Feb. 13-14	1 SA MR	rearguard, retreat to Arundel
Feb. 14-15	NSW L, NSW AMC, 1 QMI	at relief of Kimberley
Feb. 18	NSW L, NSW MR, 1 Aust. Horse	at Paardeburg
Feb. 27	—	surrender of Cronje
Feb. 28	Aust. Regt.	at relief of Colesburg
Feb. 28	—	Ladysmith relieved
Mar. 13	Aust. Regt.	at occupation, Bloemfontein
Mar. 15-27	Aust. Regt.	cross into OFS, advance to Fauresmith
Apr. 6	Aust. Regt.	hold last parade, Bloemfontein
Apr. 30	NSW MR, 1 TAS	at Battle of Houtnek
May 5	—	at Vet River
May 10	—	at Zand River
May 17	3 QMI	at relief of Mafeking
May 24-25	—	cross Vaal River
May 29	1, 2 VMR	engaged at Witwatersrand
May 30		Johannesburg surrenders
Apr.-June	Bushmen	arrive Beira, travel across to Marandellas to join Rhodesian Field Force
June 3-4	—	reach Pretoria
June 4	1, 2 VMR	heavily engaged, 6 Mile Spruit
June 11-12	NSW MR, 2 WA MI	charge enemy, Diamond Hill rout Botha's rearguard
July 3	4 WA IB	save guns after stiff resistance at Leeuw Kop
July 19	NSW MR, 4 SA IB, 4 WA IB	in action at Palmietfontein
July 21-22	NSW CIT. B, 3 VB, 3 QMI, 3 WA IB	in prolonged engagement at Koster River
July 24	4 SA IB, 1 WA MI	in sharp clash, Stinkhoutboom near Vredefort. Capt. N. R. Howse NSW AMC wins V.C.
Aug. 4-16	NSW Cit. B., 3 VB, 3 QMI, 3 WA IB	besieged at Elands River. hold out for 13 days against 2,500 of De la Reys' men
Aug. 15-16	NSW MR, NSW IB, 4 SA IB, 1 WA MI	in relief of Elands River. WA troops first to ride in from south-east
Sept. 1	3 TAS. IB	surrounded at Warmbad,

Patriotic strains from the band of the 1st Australian Commonwealth Horse on their departure for South Africa reminded Australians at home of their soldiers overseas.

KEY
All states are represented by initial.
L = Lancers
MR = Mounted Rifles
MI = Mounted Infantry
AMC = Army Medical Corps
IB = Imperial Bushmen
CIT. B = Citizen's Bushmen
B = Bushmen
ART = Artillery
ACH = Australian Commonwealth Horse
CONST. = Constabulary

Date	Unit	Action
Sept. 12	2 TAS. B / 3 SA B	Transvaal retire after gallant fight. Lt. G. C. E. Wylly and Tpr. J. H. Bisdee win V.C.s in action, Ottoshoop
Sept. 26	3 SA B / 2 TAS B	in action, Lichtenburg
Oct. 19	—	Kruger leaves by ship for Europe
Oct. 27	NSW MR	capture Krupp gun, Rensburg Drift
Nov. 5-7	NSW MR	in fight at Bothaville, enemy guns captured
Nov. 29	3 VB / 3 QMI / 4 QIB / 3 TAS. IB	in fight with Ben Viljoen's commando, Rhenoster Kop
Nov. 30	—	Lord Kitchener made CinC
Dec.	NSW Art. / 3 TAS. IB	chase de Wet in Hopetoun District

1901

Date	Unit	Action
Jan. 26	NSW IB	in action, Vlakfontein
Feb. 11	4 VIB	surprise enemy, Philipstown
Feb. 23	NSW Art. / 4 VIB / 4 QIB	capture de Wet's wagons and Maxims north of Pompean Pan
Mar. 24	NSW IB	capture De la Rey's convoy including 9 guns
Apr. 8	Bushmen	at capture of Pietersburg
Apr. 8	NSW IB	capture convoy of Kemp and Smuts, Palmietfontein
May 15-16	5, 6 WA MI	in severe fight, Brackpan, Lt. F. W. Bell wins V.C.
May 24	NSW MR	capture Potgeiter's convoy
June 6	5, 6 SA IB	in early morning march to capture de Wet's convoy.
June 12	5 VMR	camp rushed by Boers at Wilmansrust. Severe losses.
June 15	STH. AFR. CONST.	Sgt. J. Rogers (ex 1VMR) wins V.C. at Thaba 'Nchu OFS.
July 13	6 QIB	surprise laager at Koffeyfontein
July 29	5, 6 SA IB	attack Smuts at Grootvalliers Farm with fixed bayonets
Aug. 13	4 TAS. IB	fight at Roodepoort, Commdt. Erasmus captured.
Aug. 20	3 NSW IB	in 80-km night march to Wolmaranstad
Oct. 25	3 NSW MR	attempt to take Louis Botha, capture documents
Oct. 27	3 NSW IB	engage Muller's commando at Kaultsfont Nek
Oct. 30	Scottish Horse	in gallant defence of convoy at Bakenlaagte
Oct. 30	5, 6 SA IB	ride 120-km in 22 hours to relief of Bakenlaagte
Nov. 23	5 VMR	Lt. L. C. Maygar wins V.C. at Geelhoutboom

1902

Date	Unit	Action
Jan. 4	5 QIB	defend guns, Onverwacht
Jan. 4	5 VMR	at relief of Onverwacht
Feb.	—	extensive drives
Feb. 23	3 NSW MR	bring heavy fire to bear supporting NZ s near Vrede
Mar.	ACH	arrive and take part in drives
Mar. 11	2 NSW MR	in night march, Doornek
May 10	ACH	subjected to attacks as Boers try to break through line
May 31	—	Peace Treaty signed
June-Aug	—	units return to Australia and disband

On August 12, De la Rey sent another offer of honourable surrender and to that Colonel Hore replied, "Even if I wished to surrender to you — and I don't — I am commanding Australians who would cut my throat if I accepted your terms."

The fighting began again, just as heavily, but two messengers had got clear. One, from Colonel Hore to Baden-Powell, got through the Boer lines to Mafeking, which he reached on August 13; the other, from De la Rey to de Wet, was captured by a British patrol, and so headquarters discovered from two sources that the garrison had neither yielded nor been taken. Kitchener himself, trying to pin down the ever-elusive de Wet, swung away to lead his own relief column. He rode into the battered little position on the afternoon of August 16, by which time the Boers had prudently withdrawn, having seen his force approaching. Kitchener looked about and said, "Only colonials could have held out and survived in such impossible circumstances."

They had been outnumbered by four or five to one, they had been massively out-gunned, and they had never shown the slightest sign of giving in. They had lost hugely in horses, 1,400 of the 1,550 in the post being killed or dying of wounds. Among the men the casualties had been astonishingly light. Of the total of 75

General Christiaan de Wet reviews his commando, at full strength and bristling with rifles. As the British closed on Pretoria, de Wet kept up attacks on camps and supply lines.

casualties, only five were killed.

Describing the incident at Elands River, a Boer wrote, "For the first time in the war we were fighting men who used our own tactics against us. They were Australian volunteers and though small in number we could not take their position. They were the only troops who could scout into our lines at night and kill our sentries while killing and capturing our scouts. Our men admitted that the Australians were more formidable opponents and far more dangerous than any British troops."

The Transvaal had now all but fallen, it had no capital and an absent leader. Within a month, Roberts had joined with the Natal force and shaken hands with its commander, Buller, before that bluff gentleman went home. There was little formal resistance left in South Africa.

Like the Free State, the Transvaal was, again, annexed as a colony of Britain. It was all good news. In London, the government and the War Office assumed that all that was left was the mopping-up. Roberts had achieved so much that it was difficult to believe that any other real action needed to be taken. Indeed, there was some of that feeling among the Boers.

Blockhouse 75, a link in Kitchener's grid of forts and barbed wire, protects the Modder River bridge.

WITHIN THE WIRE

Kitchener's "new model drives" to clear the country were designed to offer no aid of any kind to the Boers — no home in which to rest, no sources of information, no food, or ammunition or horses with which to fight, no families to provide comfort. The heart of a nation was to be wrenched loose. Families who were, or who were suspected of being, helpful to the Boer cause, white or black, were uprooted and placed in camps. "Concentrated" was the word used. So the phrase which has developed such bitter meanings came into being.

The concentration camps housed Boer families whose men had surrendered their arms and so had to be protected from their own kind, and those whose men were still fighting and who had to be cleared from the fighting areas. Neither group received much thought or humane care; the camps were run on military lines but with reduced rations and civilian administration of the skimpiest kind — one superintendent, one doctor and a few nurses for each of the 24 camps. With food so scarce and poor, lacking vegetables and fresh milk for babies and children, sickness and disease soon took hold.

News of the camps was difficult to contain, especially as they were sited conveniently close to railway lines and so in plain view. Emily Hobhouse, a middle-aged spinster from England, heard of the camps while visiting South Africa and went to visit one. She came away appalled. She began at once to bombard Kitchener's headquarters, the press and parliament with a stream of angry letters and then, returning home, carried on her campaign in person.

By that time, the end of May 1901, more than 60,000 men, women and children were "concentrated" and out of the way as far as Kitchener was concerned. More of what he called "refugees" were pushed in every day, but the number of doctors and nurses did not rise and neither did essential supplies of medicines, bedding and food.

In London there was a great swell of revulsion when the news came out, although there were many hard-liners who maintained that speaking out against the camps was pro-Boer and treasonous. St. John Brodrick, the Under-Secretary of State for War, who had originally claimed that the camps were designed to encourage Boers to come in and surrender; that they were well designed, well-run refuges, now admitted that the camps existed purely for military reasons and that although there had been problems of administration these were being dealt with.

Emily Hobhouse countered Brodrick in a widely published report in which she described the Bloemfontein camp: "The shelter was totally insufficient. There was no room to move and the atmosphere was indescribable. There was no soap provided and the water supply would not go round. No mattresses were to be had, fuel was scanty and when the ration did not come up to the scale it became a starvation rate." And when she went back to South Africa she found that the promised improvements had been overwhelmed by the influx of new inhabitants, the camp population having doubled in a few weeks.

Meanwhile the concentration camp issue had become a focus for pro- and anti-government oratory in parliament. Lloyd George, fluent and passionate, thundered: "When children are being treated in this way and dying, we are simply ranging the deepest passions of the human heart against British rule in Africa." In August 1901, accurate figures arrived from the Cape: there were 93,940 whites imprisoned and 24,457 blacks; deaths from May to July alone numbered 3,007, and Kitchener, aware of the political implications of the camps, was even suggesting deportation for the refugees. The government was finally moved to set up a committee of enquiry headed by Mrs. Millicent Fawcett, an ardent feminist and suffragette leader. The worst of the camps on which the Fawcett Committee reported was at Mafeking where, in November 1901, the death rate from disease, including typhoid, was an appalling 400 a month.

The shocked but reasoned structure of the Fawcett Report finally brought change, and not before time. Measles, typhoid, dysentery, malnutrition and a dozen other medical conditions had brought death in the concentration camps to at least 20,000 whites and 12,000 Africans. The desolation within the wire matched the barrenness of the land outside from which the Boer families had been forcibly removed. Commando leader Jan Christiaan Smuts painted the entire picture when he wrote in his diary, "Dams everywhere full of rotting animals; water undrinkable. Veldt covered with slaughtered herds of sheep and goats, cattle and horses. The horror passes description. Surely such outrages on man and nature will lead to certain doom."

Except that Botha was still at large, as were the other swift and successful commando leaders: Smuts, De la Rey, Danie Theron, and, of course, Christiaan de Wet. It was de Wet, especially, who kept alive the Boers' hopes and their determination. He simply refused to stop fighting, to stop darting in, drawing blood and disappearing. He ambushed convoys, took an astonishing number of prisoners — 500 Yeomanry in one raid, an entire battalion of the Derbyshire Militia in another — and made a speciality of destroying railway tracks and taking supply trains and then destroying them. In a letter home, one of the soliders on de Wet's trail wrote: "He is, they say, extremely amusing, and keeps his men always in good temper with his jests; the other day, after one of his many train captures, he sent a message to the base to say that 'he was sufficiently supplied with stores now and would they kindly send up some remounts'."

Yet this extremely amusing man, when he received a letter from his brother Piet, who had surrendered, advising him to take the same course, flogged the courier who brought the letter. Then he wrote to his brother warning him that if he caught up with him he would shoot him like a dog.

The Phantom, just the inspiration the still-willing Boers needed, caused Roberts a great deal of worry. Behind the British field marshal were the conquered territories and the occupied cities and towns, but there was a huge amount of land to hold, even with his greatly expanded army. And that army was being whittled away. Many of its men, British and colonial, were volunteers who had signed for a specific period of overseas service, usually a one-year term. As those men became time-expired, so the army became that much smaller, but with no less country to cover.

In that country, the Boers still ran pretty much as they wished, moving back into any part of it, any little town or village, as the British moved through on patrol or back to a base. The big towns were the only places where army security held; outside, the country and its vulnerable rail and road communications were always at risk. Not that the military was safe: a member of one Boer commando, Denys Reitz, later described a fierce attack on a British cavalry post in which he took part. He and his fellow riders, dressed in captured khaki uniforms, killed or wounded 70-odd troopers for the loss of one dead and six wounded. Reitz went on to tell how the commando had re-equipped itself from the savaged Lancers: "We had ridden into action that morning at our last gasp and we emerged refitted from head to heel — fresh horses, fresh rifles and more ammunition than we could carry away. We were like giants refreshed."

The risk of episodes of that kind and worse grew as the Boers brought in a new tactic, cutting down the size of their commandos and developing small units with specialist skills like lightning night raids, dynamiting rail-lines, infiltrating base positions, and arson. Most important was the use of telegraphic skills for, while it was valuable to cut Roberts' links with the widespread arms of his command, it was even more valuable to leave them intact and intercept the messages the fragile wires carried.

In all that they did they had the protective colouration of the countryside. It was their land and they were part of it. A Boer soldier had only to hide his rifle and bandolier and he was again a farmer; when he was in action, virtually every civilian in his area was part of his intelligence service, catering corps, medical corps, supply echelon and camouflage.

In those six months towards the end of 1900 there were three separate types of war going on, and one was being fought in Britain. That was the political front, the battle which was leading to what became known as "The Khaki Election". Pro-Boer sentiment, stirred by young firebrands like Lloyd George, gained some quick support and some surprising opposition; by and large, the academics and students of the country joined heartily in pro-war, anti-Boer sentiments touted so strongly in the press and the parliament. The anti-war faction had little chance against a government and a majority of

British supply wagons are hauled across the dry, dusty bed of the Zand River, hot on the trail of de Wet's bold strike south into Cape Colony.

the people who wanted the Boers put down. In their eyes the war was a rebellion against the Crown; southern Africa, all of it, rightly belonged to Britain, and they wanted the rebels punished and the disputed territories brought back into the Empire. The same pro-war sentiments were also strong in Australia, where the public's enthusiasm had been fuelled by press reports of the success of Diamond Hill and the courage of local troops at Elands River.

Then there was the "proper" military front of the war, the front on which fought Roberts and Kitchener and the regulars, who saw their duty plainly: to follow the government's orders, to pass those orders down the line and to see that they were carried out, no matter what the difficulties.

The third kind of war was, as 1900 passed its mid-mark, something else again. It was the beginning of a much more savage kind of campaign altogether, and Australians were to play an unpleasantly prominent part in it.

Roberts was ready to go home, but not before seeing his final campaign move into its fully operational phase. He was old and had taken a fall from a horse and broken an arm, but he was the same tough and uncompromising soldier and leader who had ridden with his troops all the way from Bloemfontein to Pretoria. He now began the active stages of his plan for finishing off the war which he had told London was as good as over. It was the plan whose first tentative phase had drawn from Lloyd George the bitter statement: "A war of annexation against a proud people must be a war of extermination, and that is unfortunately what it seems we are now committing ourselves to."

The basis of the plan was simple. Mark off the maps of Boer territory in grid-squares to show where "protected areas" could be established, then translate the pencil marks into roughly surveyed points on the land. Within each square build blockhouses, each in rifle-range of the next, and run barbed wire from every blockhouse to the next in each direction, so enclosing the open veldt in an interlocking system of

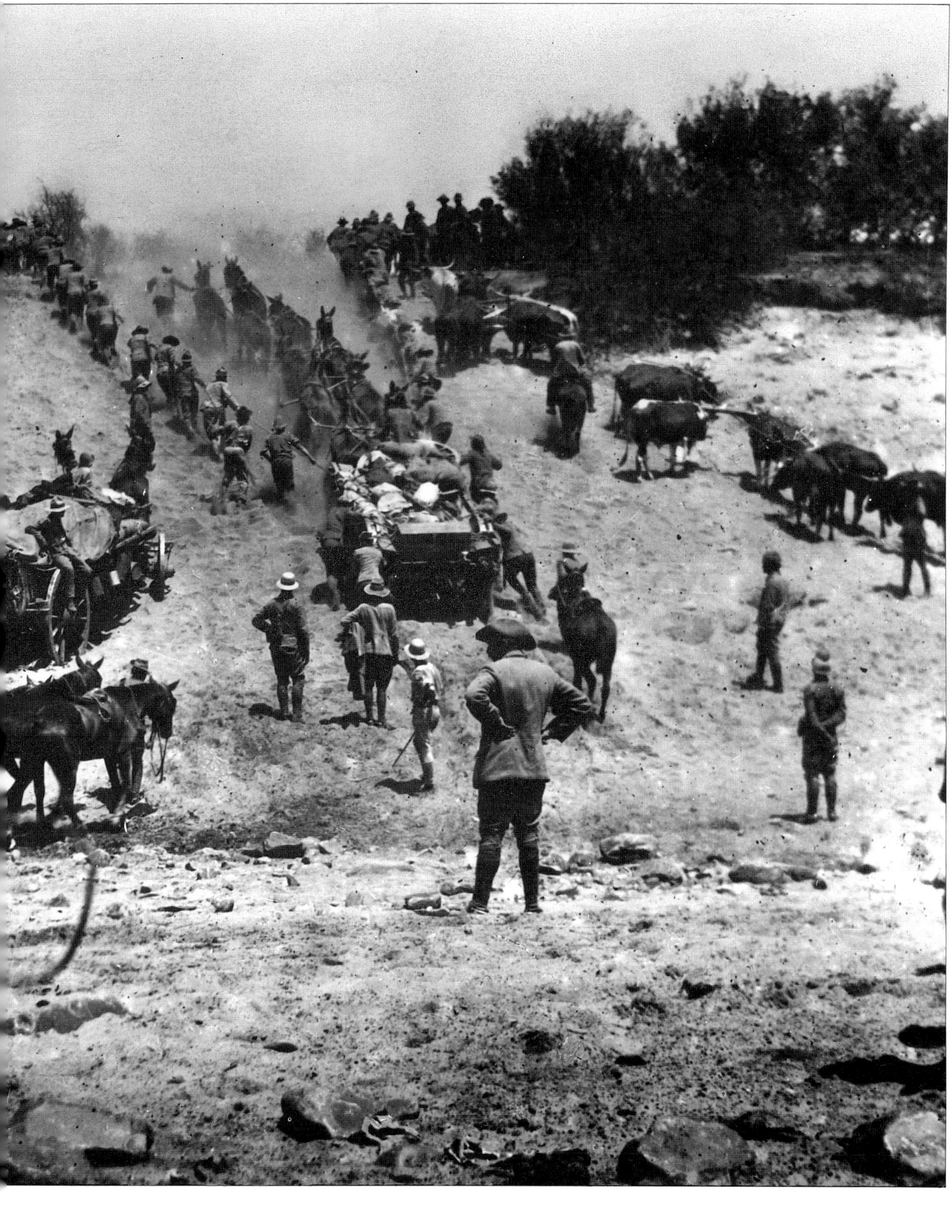

armed squares. Then, quite deliberately, one grid-square at a time, turn out the occupants of farms, tiny settlements, and crossway trade-stores, and burn the buildings to the ground. Drive off the livestock, poison the wells, trample any growing crops and take the occupants away, out of that square, and concentrate them somewhere else. One grid-square at a time, absolutely deny the Boer his essential local suppliers of food and intelligence and hideaways. Clear and totally despoil a square and move on. In Biblical times it was called "sowing the land with salt".

In such fashion, the year 1900 drew to its increasingly miserable and bitter close. Despite the volunteers leaving and the regular units being posted home again, there was still a significant force in South Africa. The army which had started with 10,000 men, still had, even in its diminished state, more than 200,000 men on strength. The Boers available to join commandos had shrunk by more than half, and they were without some leaders, without major bases and were being forced more and more away from the help of their countrymen. Yet there were still leaders loose and there were still about 30,000 commando men, armed and mounted, in the Free State.

By the beginning of November, with Kruger in France, Christiaan de Wet, the Phantom himself, suffered an inglorious defeat at the hands of an inferior British force. Camped with President Steyn at Bothaville on the Valsch River, in the curve of an arc down and west from Pretoria to Bloemfontein, he and his 800 men were caught napping — literally. His own tactics were used against him when 600 men of the advance guard of a column under Major-General Charles Knox came out of the night, found the outposts and sentries asleep and at once attacked. Had the main column come up faster there is no doubt that de Wet and Steyn would have been captured. As it was, a heroic rearguard stand enabled them to get away once again, but de Wet lost all his artillery and the entire rearguard, 25 killed and 130 captured, many of them wounded.

On November 29, Roberts handed over command to Kitchener and began his journey home to an old-fashioned triumph, in which parliament, press and people joined to salute him and shower him with gifts including a peerage and £100,000. He arrived back in England in December, and was summoned to visit the aged and ailing Queen, taking the sea air on the Isle of Wight. It was as well he went when he did, for Victoria of England died on January 22, 1901.

Exactly three weeks earlier, the Australian colonies had achieved a new status. On January 1, 1901, those colonies became a federation of states, a Commonwealth. Australia was a nation.

FROM REDCOAT TO KHAKI

British troops garrisoned in Australia from the 1790s wore the distinctive "redcoat" which became synonymous with British soldiery throughout the Empire. Along with the Empire's expansion in the last half of the 19th century, its soldiers were glorified in paintings and respected the world over, yet despite such impressions, the regular British trooper was far from being a strapping example of the Mother Country's manhood.

He was a very short fellow. His average height of 160 centimetres (5 feet, 3 inches) in 1883 dropped to a diminutive 152 cm (5 feet) in 1900. This was possibly because he came from sickly and undernourished stock, the British army recruiting largely from its country's unemployed, poor, and criminal classes. A soldier's life offered him regular pay, food, and a place to sleep which was an attractive alternative to the cramped, squalid, and stifling conditions in Britain's urban and rural slums. Not the least of the attractions of army life was an impressive uniform in which even a short, stocky foot soldier cut a dashing figure.

The British soldier in Australia wore his redcoat with a tall, black leather helmet, or shako, surmounted by a white pompon, the typical headgear of the British regiments, with brass badge on each helmet bearing the regiment's number. It was superseded by a German-style leather or canvas helmet with its characteristic spike. The red stripe down the blue serge trouser leg was a symbolic vestige of the days when a cavalry officer would wipe his blood-stained sword across his thigh in the thick of battle.

On campaign, with 60 rounds of ammunition, clothes, a bag of rations, blanket and waterbottle, a private of the 58th Regiment would carry up to 32 kilograms on his back. He holds an Enfield percussion rifle, successor to the famous Brown Bess musket.

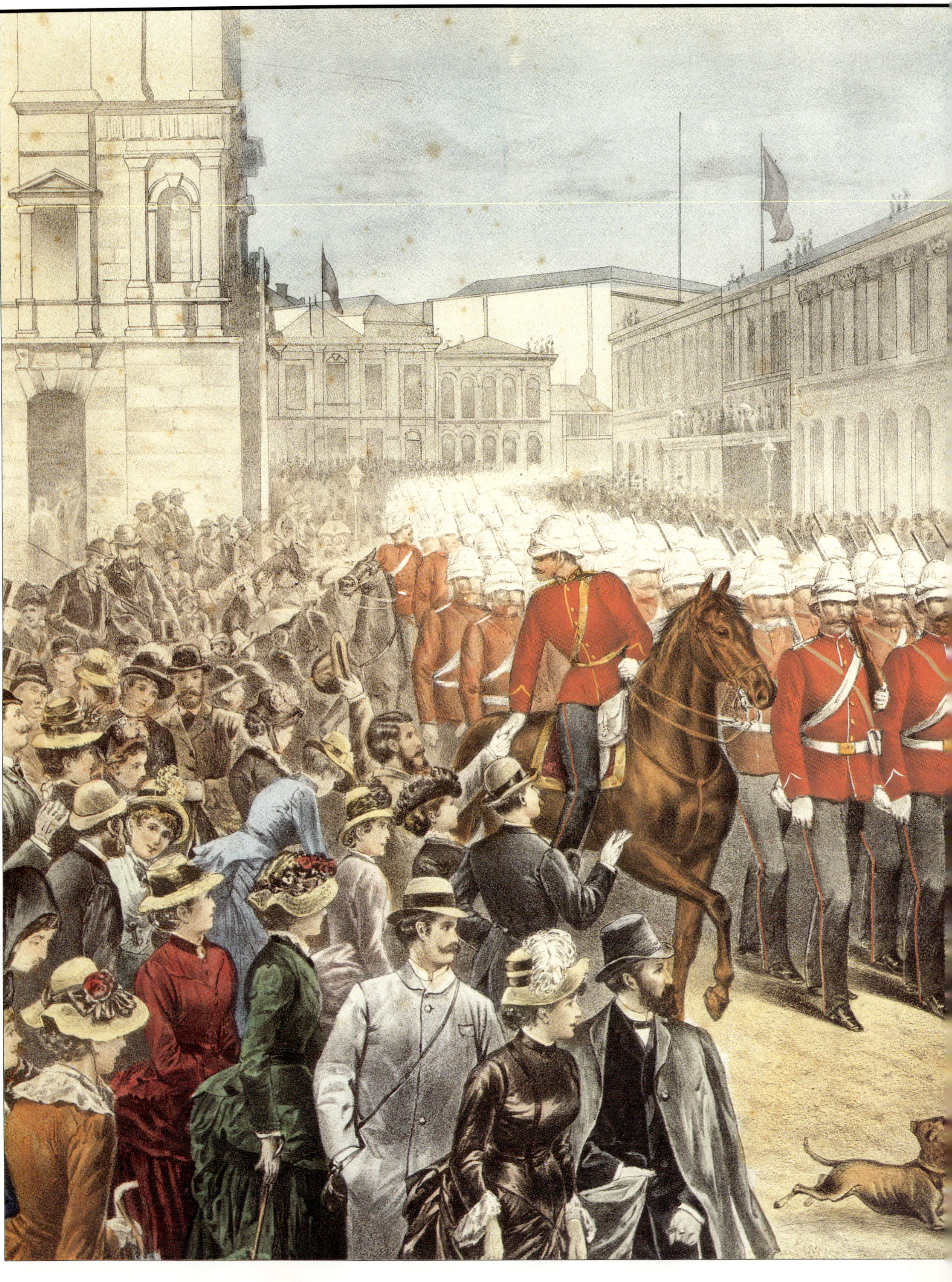

Australia's volunteers to the Sudan were uniformed like this private of the old 58th Regiment, which amalgamated in 1881 with the 48th to become the Northamptonshire Regiment. He is armed with a Lee-Metford magazine rifle and wearing a spiked German-style leather helmet. On overseas service in the tropics, the helmet would be white, as shown in the painting (left) of the enthusiastic departure of the NSW contingent for the Sudan. Despite the unknown artist's spirited scene, the painting inaccurately shows the soldier's wide tunic strap worn over the left shoulder, when correctly, it should be over the right shoulder.

147

The Australian mounted infantryman on the veldt, already as khaki as the South African countryside around him and dressed for convenience. His rifle is still the efficient eight-shot Lee-Metford and he carries a bandolier of .303 ammunition for it. Behind him is a signals detachment using a heliograph and the sun's rays to flash a morse message to a distant unit.

A SOLDIER EVOLVES

During the 1860s and 1870s the colonial governments began to raise their own local infantry, artillery and mounted units, with uniforms closely modelled on their British counterparts. When the Waikato Regiment was formed to fight in New Zealand in 1863, volunteer forces from the different colonies assembled in a bizarre medley of military costume, but were issued with silver-trimmed scarlet tunics, silver, lace-trimmed, grey trousers and grey caps. This finery was swapped for blue shirt and trousers, soft forage cap, and short boots and leggings for action in the field.

A similarly motley-uniformed force lined up on the parade ground at Victoria Barracks in Sydney for the Sudan contingent in 1885, but they were soon decked out in traditional red tunic, blue trousers and white helmet, with its spike replaced by a white button. Cuffs and collars were blue and piped in white, while the officers and NCOs were distinguished by rank badges, silver braid and lace on cuffs, collars and shoulder straps. This spectacularly colourful outfit was only worn for the ceremonial departure and in the Sudan the Australians were given a far more practical khaki cotton jacket and trousers. A cloth veil, or puggaree, behind the helmet provided protection from the sun and long canvas gaiters stopped sand creeping into boots. The artillerymen kept their dark-blue uniform, but often adopted a so-called "mushroom" sun helmet.

When the marine detachment was raised for the China expedition in 1899, the force had to be clothed and equipped at short notice. The sailors were fitted for their serge-blue jackets and cloth-covered leather caps only days before embarkation and the NSW Naval Brigade arrived in Peking still wearing old-fashioned panama-style straw hats. The Marine Light Infantry, diverted from the third contingent to South Africa, retained their forage caps, khaki uniforms and slouch hats for parade dress.

The slouch hat, originally a fashion accessory was adapted for use in the British and Indian armies after 1850. The uniquely Australian aspect of the slouch hat has been its turned-up brim at the side. The Victorian Mounted Rifles were probably the first to establish this practice by pinning the brim up on the right-hand side. Other Australian units followed suit, but by time of the Boer War the hat more commonly had its brim turned up on the left-hand side, which made it easier to carry a rifle sloped over the left shoulder. The khaki felt slouch hat with the Rising Sun badge on its upturned brim was to become the single most powerful symbol of Australia's fighting men.

In the Boer War, the Australian soldier was no longer dressed as an integral part of the British war machine, although dress uniforms were still inspired by British sartorial extravagance. Some infantry officers still wore camouflaged pith helmets. The Australian Light Horse boasted a smart, myrtle-green uniform. The NSW Lancers and NSW Mounted Rifles sported an emu feather plume atop their slouch hats and carried cavalry swords. Increasingly, however, the Australian soldier, fighting and living on the South African veldt, came to resemble the Boer enemy. In dun-coloured khaki jacket and trousers, long puttees and wearing a beaten-up slouch hat or Bushman's hat (copied directly from the Boer), the Australians dressed sensibly for the climate, the environs and the campaign. His highly individual mode of dress, casual by military standards, distinguished him from the British regular and also expressed a marked difference in temperament and fighting style.

It was in the Boer War that the Australian trooper's skills as a horseman, marksman and bushman came to the fore and earned him the reputation of an adaptable, fit and effective fighting man. He was not only better dressed for this campaign than his British cousin, but more physically suited. He was taller, lankier and more healthy. It was in this war that a strong creed of mateship and a healthy scepticism towards unthinking obedience to orders and authoritarian leadership measured the distance between the Australian soldier and his British comrade, and were to become features of an Australian tradition — the Digger tradition.

The Australian soldier would swap his slouch hat for a Tommy tin helmet in a later war, but he would forever wear the uniform of the Australian Army. He had evolved from a colonial Redcoat to a khaki-clad Australian soldier.

150 *Australian and New Zealand mounted troops show their superb horsemanship, even as they face the enemy at Klerksdorp, March 24, 1901. Klerksdorp*

became Kitchener's base as he sought to crush Boer commando leader Koos De la Rey. (Charles Hammond, 1904.)

One of the most famous Australian paintings of a solider in battle or in peacetime is this portrait of Sergeant R.D. Fraser of the NSW Mounted Rifles. The artist is the celebrated painter Tom Roberts, who completed this work in 1896.

British artist Richard Simkin's colour lithograph was one of a series on uniforms for an Australian military gazette in 1900. The two equestrian officers on the left belong to the NSW Lancers and wear dress uniform (front) and ceremonial review uniform (behind). On the right are (on horseback) a NSW Mounted Rifles officer in review uniform and (standing) two NSW Field Artillery officers in dress uniform.

153

6

ENDGAME

As the Boers crumbled under Kitchener's brutal campaign of destruction, Australian soldiers were prey to the harsh political realities of Empire. From then on, the new Commonwealth of Australia made ready to stand and fight on its own.

To the men on the way home, the new Australia might have had great significance. The unification, at least the proclaiming of unification, of a group of separate colonial places into a single Commonwealth may have made them feel different in some way, perhaps in some way better than when they had left.

To the men still in the field there was no apparent change. They were still under British command and it would not be until 1902 that they would be joined by the proudly named Australian Commonwealth Horse. The work, too, remained the work they had been doing all along. They became part of Kitchener's meticulously planned and cold-blooded clearing of the land, which became increasingly concentrated as it took on the dispassionate name of the "new model drives".

While column after column chased de Wet around and across the Free State, thousands of other men, Australians included, were put to the hateful business of scorching the good South African earth.

By the first week of November 1901, the protected areas which had begun as map markings were, in fact, 26,000 square kilometres of the Transvaal and the north of the Free State, and

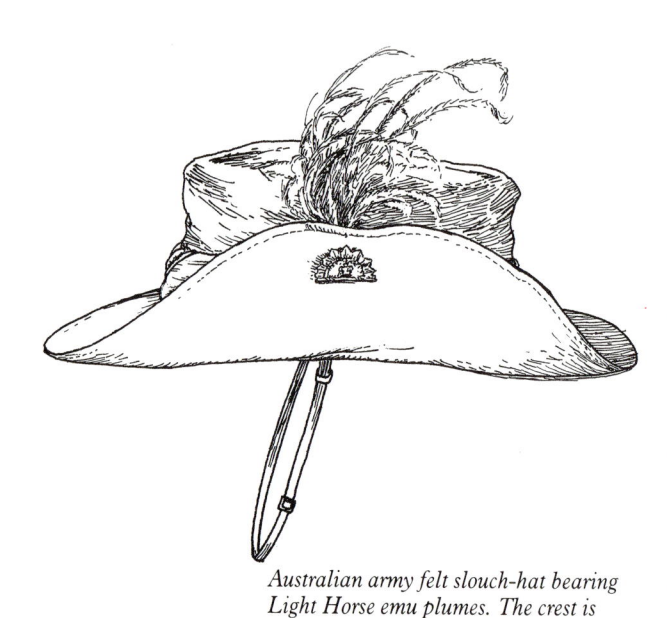

Australian army felt slouch-hat bearing Light Horse emu plumes. The crest is the Australian army insignia, the Rising Sun.

another 10,000 square kilometres around Bloemfontein. Those great tracts were declared to be absolutely clear of Boer fighting men. Inside the grid-squares the soldiers had moved, thousands of them spaced 10 or 15 metres apart in lines, beaters driving human game up against barbed wire and blockhouses, destroying the land as they passed across it. For the men from Australia, New Zealand, and Canada, it was an especially unpleasant thing to do; they were largely men who knew the difficulty of taming the land and making it produce and give value, and to take part in its destruction was bitterly distasteful for them. Under orders, they searched farms and little stores for weapons, watched as women and children and old men loaded what they could onto carts and supervised their enforced movement to concentration camps. Their cattle and goats and poultry were taken for the pot, and what was left of their homes was looted as often as not and then burnt.

But that was within those protected areas, within the established and sterilised spaces. Away from them, in the wild country, there were still grim-faced fighters, mounted, armed, seasoned and efficient. From a distance, those men of the commandos saw the smoke go up from burning houses and crops and grassland and watched as families were taken away. Sometimes they were close enough to hear the crying of the children above the crackle of the burning. Those fires lit a different kind of flame among the Boer men.

Roberts was right when he said that the war was over. The kind of war he had fought, of set-piece battles and march-countermarch, was over. Now, in 1901, the soldiers of the new nation of Australia found themselves in another kind of war entirely. Savage, vengeful and without quarter, this was, on the one side, what Lloyd George had said in the British Parliament, a war of extermination; and on the other, it was a guerrilla war. In it, Australia's soldiers were credited with great work, but the nation's name would be blackened. And the new Commonwealth would take an adult step away from Mother England.

The men who had served longest in South Africa had absorbed lessons which the army had not taught, but which the Boers had. The early feeling about fighting "native rebels" had long gone; it had become one of respect for the enemy's ability as a fighting man, if not, in the British sense, as a soldier. But there was an undertone of frustration and resentment towards it all. The men fighting the Boer felt they had spent too long in trying to put down an opponent who seemed impossible to crush, no matter how many times he was beaten. They sensed that many of the civilians among whom they moved and sometimes lived were against them, passively when observed, actively whenever it became possible. There had been many farmers who had concealed their weapons when being searched, but who fired on troops when they turned their backs. Often, too, farmers would fly a white flag but shoot any soldier who fell for the ruse. There was a sense of outrage at fighting men who often wore captured British uniforms, who fired British ammunition from captured army guns, and who sometimes stripped prisoners and sent them back to their own lines naked. The Boers did not fight like gentlemen, but with a ferocity that knew no rules. They were fighting in and for their own land, fighting for their homes and beliefs and livelihood against an invader. They had nothing to lose by going on with the fight as bitterly as they could against greatly superior numbers, despite divisions and desertions and derelictions among their own politicians and people. As they began to suffer deeply from Kitchener's policy, as their support and supplies began to dwindle, so their bitterness deepened. Their actions in the field began to be harsher and they found a greater need to arm and equip and feed themselves from the British forces and whoever supported them.

Wars tend to breed military mimicries. Successful units soon enough find themselves being countered by similar forces on the other side in the way that new weapons are offset by new defences. In South Africa, the Boer style of combat was recognised, after too long, perhaps, as best suited to the terrain and the outcome was the call for more and more Mounted Infantry and Mounted Rifles, men who could ride hard, live rough, and fight well, just as the Boers did. It was a call well and successfully answered by the men from Australia. And when the Boers began to split their commandos into smaller, more specialised units, the inevitable result was that the British army did the same.

There had been small and individual units operating as part of the army almost since the outbreak of the war. Some of them were no more than sections of scouts recruited locally and used in much the same way that the United States Cavalry in the Old West had used local Indians. Some were Boers who either did not believe in the Boer cause or could see no future, or profit, in it.

On the far forward edges of Kitchener's clearing operations, up in the rocky heights above the veldt and out along the farthest stretches of the railway lines, both sides were fighting more brutally, caring less about taking prisoners, and not especially worrying about putting wounded men "out of their misery". More and more there were abuses of flags of truce; less and less were such flags, or any other civilised conventions recognised. And it was not, it was never, one-sided.

From quite early in the war, the British counter to Boer explosives under railway lines had been to couple a flat-car ahead of an engine and load it with prisoners, women and children among them. Now, with Boer families held in concentration camps, the Boer counter was, as often as not, the stripping and degrading of captives before shooting them. Sometimes the bodies would be sent back into army lines. So the stage of the war which had been reached, the time and fighting which had gone by, and the type of man who was being used, all conspired to create this new and callous warfare.

Because of their ease in the saddle and in the field, men from the outlands of the Empire were well equipped for scouting and forward work. Among them were many who had no particular desire to go home at the end of the enlistments, who were lured by the prospects of excitement, a lessening of discipline, possibly loot, and in some cases advancement. When the chance was

As part of Kitchener's drive to cut support for the Boer fighters, Imperial troops burn Boer farmhouses and crops.

offered to stay on, to re-enlist in a less regular military formation, perhaps to gain a sergeant's chevrons or a lieutenant's pips, it was often enough leapt at.

The men who joined the irregular units were likely to be much of a kind. Almost all of them were seasoned in South Africa by then. All of them were, at the least, competent horsemen and weapons managers, and, like the men they opposed, they came from many places. On the army side, too, less regular units were put together. They were composites, volunteers from a variety of regiments and countries. They were likely to dress very informally and had no regimental traditions to tie them to a code of conventions. Operating well away from any main base or headquarters, in difficult country and against an enemy of proven fighting qualities, they met fire with fire. And there erupted, beyond Kitchener's new model drives, a blaze of bitter actions, small but savage and usually marked by a great indifference towards the rules of war.

Out there, in front of the front, looting was widespread. British troops ransacked and pillaged usually for food and liquor, but if there was anything else which caught a soldier's fancy he was unlikely to leave it behind. If he found nothing he needed or wanted, he was as likely as not to destroy in anger whatever there was. The Boers in their turn had long descended on the farms and property of Britishers or their supporters and stripped and destroyed them, less wantonly perhaps, more as a calculated act of war. It was just as effective and just as painful.

Christiaan de Wet called the blockhouse system "the blockhead system", claiming that they cost many thousands of pounds and that it cost even more to feed the men manning them. He said, "And it was all money thrown away. This wonderful scheme of the English prolonged the war for at least three months." But the blockhouses, the widespread property destruction, and the concentration camps, all on top of the Boers' intense nationalism and deep religious beliefs, set the stage for this, the end-game of the war. It had degenerated from a war in which an army fought most of a nation to one in which elements of that army fought elements of that nation in outer areas. In the meantime, politicians and generals on both sides were much engaged in trying to end the whole thing, each to his own country's advantage, neither wishing to appear to have given in.

For Kitchener there were two sharp goads. He wanted to get away from South Africa to India. That prize of Empire had been held out to him and he wanted to grasp it, first in the promised post of Commander-in-Chief then, he hoped, as Viceroy. Anything which would speed this ambition was a priority for him, whether it was fighting or negotiating a peace, or both simultaneously.

The second goad was a professional military one. He was commanding an army which was, to his mind, lax and ill-disciplined. Reports came to his desk which told of irregularities of dress, behaviour, actions in the field, of inefficiencies and desertions, and to his rigid and regular mind things of that kind could not be borne. Not only were they bad for the morale of the army as a whole but they would weaken his

THE BREAKER

Harry Harbord Morant became a legend twice in his lifetime, yet arguments have raged for almost a century about who exactly he was. The dispossessed son of an English county family, as he claimed? The child of a workhouse-master in Devon? The illegitimate son of a Royal Navy admiral? No one has ever been able to say for sure, but there is certainly no dispute about his life in Australia.

He arrived around 1885, a short, well set-up man in his twenties, well-spoken, charming when he chose and carrying all the marks of the classic remittance man. Except for the remittance. The story which spread — undoubtedly started by Harry Morant himself — was that he had been a Royal Naval officer but had handed in his papers because of gambling debts, after which his father, an admiral, had disowned him.

Harry settled into Australia with singular ease, shrugging himself into the bushman's life as though he was pulling on a familiar coat. He worked as a roustabout, jackeroo, and fencing-hand on sheep and cattle properties in a long arc from around Charters Towers in Queensland down to Renmark in South Australia and he became well and widely known for two very different reasons. His horsemanship was remarkable. He could coax uneasy horses to jump high and difficult obstacles, he rode as though he and the horse were a single animal and he could break and gentle the fiercest brumby.

It was that skill which earned him the nickname "The Breaker" — and it was under that name that he earned the other reputation. He wrote verse — bush ballads, little satirical odes, lyrical love poems — and was published across the country in the *Bulletin* and, locally, by district newspapers like the *Richmond and Windsor Gazette*. Many times he would scribble off some light doggerel in exchange for a drink.

As Regimental Number 37, Lance-Corporal H.H. Morant sailed with the 2nd South Australian Mounted Rifles in January 1900 and landed at the Cape on February 25 to begin the last two years of his life. He was a good and efficient soldier, skilled at the

Harry Harbord Morant.

military arts of movement and fighting in rough country and just as skilled in finding easy tasks whenever he could. His value as a horseman was multiplied when he "scrounged" or "found" horses of fine quality for staff officers — and often enough stole them back for resale.

When Harry's enlistment period was up, he went on leave to Britain, where he became friends with Hussar officer, Captain Frederick Hunt.

Both men cut short their leave and returned to the Cape to take commissions in a newly formed and irregular unit called the Bush Veldt Carbineers, the BVC, which operated in the rough and broken country north of Pietersburg. The set-piece battles of the war were by now over and the Boers were fighting a desperate and deadly guerrilla war; the BVC fought back on the same terms, bitterly and savagely. Given that they were neither regular soldiers nor particularly good men, it is hardly surprising that "irregularities" were common. When, in August 1901, Hunt was killed and appeared to have been mutilated by Boers, Harry Morant went quietly berserk at his friend's death, and over the next two months carried out a series of savage raids in which Boers taken prisoner were summarily shot.

On one occasion a German missionary, Dr. Heese, was stopped by a patrol led by Morant and saw the corpses of eight Boer prisoners, including an old man and a child. When Heese was shortly afterwards found shot to death, six BVC officers were arrested and variously charged with looting, manslaughter and the missionary's murder. The court of enquiry recommended court martial.

Of the six men charged, one, the commanding officer, was reprimanded and sent home to Australia, his career shattered. A second, the intelligence officer, escaped entirely as he had by then left the service and was no longer subject to military law. The only regular British officer charged, Harry Picton, was cashiered and sank into obscurity; the other three were sentenced to death — although none was found guilty of the murder of the missionary. One sentence was commuted to life imprisonment and that man, George Witton, served almost four years in British gaols before a petition secured his release. The other two men were Peter Handcock, a railway blacksmith from Bathurst and Harry Morant's devoted follower, and Morant himself.

On the morning of Feburary 27, 1902, a firing-party shot them to death — and Morant, bushman, balladist and horse-master passed into Australian legend as The Breaker.

Peter Handcock (far left), Harry Morant (patting dog), Frederick Hunt (third from right) and Harry Picton (far right).

THE PRISONER'S FRIEND

That old British army term for an officer speaking in defence of an accused soldier was very apt for James Francis Thomas, country lawyer, volunteer-soldier and friend to the death.

Thomas was a farmer's son, born in 1861 a little west of Sydney and with a brain good enough to take him from the land and earn him a law degree from the University of Sydney. Nonetheless he had no desire to settle in the city and, as soon as his articled time had been served, he moved to the far north of New South Wales and, in 1890, established a practice in Tenterfield, in the rich and well-watered New England area. He was a 2nd Lieutenant serving with the Tenterfield Company, Mounted Infantry Regiment.

By the outbreak of the Boer War Thomas was, at 38, a successful solicitor and an influential man. As the owner of the local newspaper, the *Tenterfield Star*, he carried considerable weight in the political field; he was outspokenly in favour of the federation of the colonies, for decentralisation and for a separate state of New England. And by 1899 he commanded the district's Volunteers.

James Francis Thomas.

In February 1900, Major J. F. Thomas, Officer Commanding 'A' Squadron of the NSW Bushmen's Contingent, sailed with his men for South Africa. He did well in the field, serving in a number of actions, including the Relief of Mafeking, and earned the Queen's South Africa Medal with four campaign clasps. And then, suddenly, he found himself at law again.

One of the Bush Veldt Carbineers arraigned for a court martial was the Commanding Officer, Major Robert Lenehan, also a lawyer in civilian life. The suggestion has been made that he particularly requested Thomas' legal assistance and, indeed, it is possible that they had met professionally before the war. However it came about, Thomas, accepted by the court, found himself defending all the accused men.

His clients had already been subjected to 12 weeks of close, generally solitary, confinement, and had been through a rigorous court of enquiry. They had had practically no time for consultation with this unknown major of Mounted Infantry who was to defend them — and he knew almost nothing about them except the charges against them.

Moreover, Thomas was a country lawyer with no civil trial experience, let alone a military trial concerned with capital charges. That he did so well is a tribute to his intelligence, his skill and his plain conviction that an injustice was being done.

He pleaded cogently and successfully enough to get Major Lenehan no more than a reprimand and to get the others acquitted entirely on one charge. And when the court came to sentencing it was Thomas' pleading which caused three recommendations for mercy. But there was no way he could clear them all of every charge, no way he could save Peter Handcock and Breaker Morant from that row of rifles.

Back again in Tenterfield, Thomas began a personal and public campaign to push the point that two men had been shot and another imprisoned for doing no more than hundreds of others had done throughout the war. In a passionate letter to the Bathurst newspaper, the *National Advocate*, on April 2, 1902, he wrote, "It was proved that in other cases exactly the same procedure was adopted and approved of by other officers. As counsel I should like to see that all the facts from the prisoners' point of view are fairly brought forward." It was an attitude from which he never departed.

He took up again the running of his law practice and his newspaper, his association with volunteer military activities and became trustee and patron of the Mounted Rifle Club and an accomplished fund-raiser for ex-servicemen's needs. But he was obsessed by what had happened in South Africa and devoted much of his time and intellect to righting the perceived wrong — so much so that his other work suffered and he ran into considerable debt.

He developed a strong aversion to what he saw as government interference in his personal affairs and he consistently refused to submit his accounts for taxation assessment. There was also some suspicion that he handled clients' trust funds a little loosely, but it was the taxation matter which eventually saw him imprisoned in Long Bay Gaol in 1928. He was released a year later, declared bankrupt and unable to practise law. He returned to Tenterfield where he died on November 11, Armistice Day, 1942, aged 81.

situation if he had to sit down with Boer leaders and talk terms. He determined to be as hard on his own men as he had been on the enemy's, and in early 1902 he had the chance to prove to his army that he meant business.

One of the irregular units which had sprung up in the north, in the area known as the Spelonken, was called the Bush Veldt Carbineers, a rag-tag-and-bobtail collection of hard cases and bad hats, British, South African and Australian. Among its officers was Harry "the Breaker" Morant, the poet and horseman who had become a soldier as brutal as any other. He and the men with whom he rode were undoubtedly as guilty as hundreds, perhaps thousands, of others; they had shot prisoners, shot wounded men, looted and destroyed without doubt.

It was not until a German missionary was shot to death in their area that six of them were brought to trial, four of them for his murder, but they were cleared on that charge for lack of proof. There was enough proof for the rest of their crimes, manslaughter and the murder of Boer prisoners, and not even an impassioned defence by Lieutenant James Francis Thomas, once an officer in the Upper Clarence Light Horse, could convince the court that they were no guiltier than much of the rest of the army. They had just had the very bad luck to be the ones caught and tried.

An ex-Intelligence officer arrested with them got clean away because his service time was up and the military court no longer had jurisdiction over him. Their commanding officer was sent back to Australia with a reprimand and a scarred career. The only British regular officer among the principal four accused was cashiered and one of the others, sentenced to death, had his sentence commuted to life imprisonment. The remaining two, Morant and his friend, Lieutenant Peter Handcock, were sentenced to death and executed on February 27, 1902.

During the courts of enquiry and right through to the court martial, cold-hearted politicking had gone on behind the scenes and the fighting had remained tough at the front. Australians had ridden with General John French when he led eight columns into East Transvaal against Louis Botha and from January to March 1901, hustled him and his elusive commandos.

In the middle of the chase, on the last day of February 1901, action was suspended so that Botha and Kitchener could actually meet, in a railway carriage at Middelburg, to discuss possible peace terms. The talks proved useless, conceivably not helped by the massacre by Jan Smuts's commando of all the natives at a town called Modderfontein and by Christiaan de Wet slipping through the guards along the Orange River and taking his men on a raid into Cape Colony. Botha went back to the fight, and within a fortnight of the end of the talks the first big drives began in the north of the Orange Free State.

Australian troops met with their worst disaster of the war in this period. A detachment of the 5th Victorian Mounted Rifles, sweeping through east Transvaal, were camped near Wilmansrust, south of Middelburg, when they were infiltrated on June 12 by a large commando of Boers. The enemy had got through inadequate pickets placed by the Imperial officer commanding them, Major Morris, who had also ordered all rifles to be stacked in piles according strictly to drill regulations. Such a practice was unwise against the lightning strikes of the Boers, and the Victorians were soundly defeated, losing 20 men with 40 more wounded.

The Australians were later rebuked by the British commander of the region, Major-General S.B. Beatson, and this was followed by a threat to mutiny among the Victorian ranks, who placed the blame for their losses squarely on their British officers. Three men were sentenced to death, but their sentences were commuted by Kitchener. The whole affair followed-up the Morant and Handcock executions and further hardened Australian attitudes toward British military law.

Still, Kitchener's blockhouse-and-barbed-wire system went remorselessly ahead and the drives went with it, to the end of 1901 and beyond. On Christmas Day, appropriately not far from a settlement called Bethlehem, the

Kitchener (seated second from right) and his staff meet with General Botha (seated to his right) and staff for peace talks at Middelburg in February 1901. The talks stalemated and war continued.

irrepressible de Wet struck a construction camp at the end of a blockhouse line and, as both sides did often enough, used cross-cut and expanding bullets as they stormed in, inflicting terrible damage, killing and seriously wounding many men and capturing piles of valuable stores.

In February, 1902, de Wet slipped away again from a major effort to catch him, and this time he took President Steyn out of the Free State, stampeding a mob of cattle ahead of them through three blockhouse lines, across the Vaal River and joining De la Rey in the west of the Transvaal. In the next month, De la Rey, raiding successfully in a wide ring around the Mafeking railway line, hit hard, successfully and bloodily at a supply convoy and then at Lord Methuen's column, mainly fresh yeomanry and irregulars. Methuen was wounded in the thigh and suffered the ignominy of being the only British general to be captured during the war.

On April 11 came the final set-piece of the war, an old-fashioned cavalry charge by the Boers at Rooiwal, the Red Valley. It came within an inch of success but the British gap closed and inflicted great punishment on those hard-fighting, long-lasting, land-loving Boers.

A week before that battle Cecil Rhodes had died. A week after it, Boer peace delegates were meeting in Pretoria, although the drives were still going on, and continued into May. It was not until the last day of May that a surrender was signed at Vereeniging. Perhaps the clearest indication of the Boer way of life was that their negotiating party was not one of practising politicians. The five men selected were, by then, known and respected across South Africa as men who upheld their religious beliefs, who had been both successful civilians and successful soldiers and now, at the last, as trusted spokesmen. They were Judge Hertzog, who had once led an invading commando into Cape Colony, General Koos De la Rey, State Attorney Jan Smuts, General Louis Botha and the Phantom, General Christiaan de Wet. When they rose from the conference table the Boer war had ended.

The Australian soliders to leave South Africa had completed an education begun in New Zealand 50 years earlier. They had found that their battlefield enemies, the Boers, were no more professional soldiers than any Australian volunteer. Like the Australians, the Boers had come from farm, shop, store and schoolroom, from vocation, profession and trade. Unlike them, the Boers had fought for their absolutes — convictions, church and country — and had succeeded in humiliating some of Britain's oldest and proudest regiments, policies and practices.

There were things to tell the people at home in this new and unified land, this Commonwealth of Australia. The people at home needed to be told, for example, that the British could be fooled, could be out-foxed, could be beaten; that the traditional, believed-in-without-question British ruling class was capable of ignorance and stupidity and simple short-sightedness just as it was capable of great bravery and extraordinary feats. It was, in other words, as fallible as any other human system.

For the returned soldier, there was another and different viewpoint, retrospective and prospective. He had seen what it was like, seen how out-of-date thinking had been forced to change under pressure; seen how his own colonial force had, by its very nature, been more competent from the start, even without centuries of tradition; seen how much more quickly he had been able to develop new ideas than had the slow-to-change British army, strapped into its harness of tradition and class separation.

The men of the Lancers, of the Mounted Infantry, the Mounted Rifles, the Volunteer Rifles, the Volunteer Artillery, the Bushmen and eventually the Australian Commonwealth Horse went from the great southland's separate colonies and states. They went back to a Commonwealth as part of a national army and the lessons they had learned were, like all of war, sweet and sour. The sweetness was a compound of comradeship and laughter and the relief of tension after battle; the sourness was an ill-coloured mixture of the blood of friend and enemy and the hard-won knowledge that mistakes and haste, and ignorance and arrogance were all likely to mean death. The aftertaste was to be carried with many of them and with their sons and younger brothers into another war.

The men who rode across the Orange Free State and the Transvaal, the men who fought in Cape Colony and Natal, set the standard for the men of Gallipoli, for the Light Horse Regiments who fought there dismounted, for those who rode across the deserts into Gaza and Damascus and in the mad and blood-stirring ride for the wells of Beersheba.

Between the Redcoats of the 58th (Rutlandshire) Regiment of Foot who fought the magnificent Maoris in the middle of the 19th century and the scruffy, bearded trooper in a forward scouting party in the Zoutpansberg of the Transvaal, there were a score of differences. There were differences of dress and diet, of arms and attitudes, of politics and principles.

Those differences, in not much more than half a century, became national characteristics, exemplified by the picture of the "digger", the larrikin in khaki who does not salute an officer he does not know, and then only when he has seen him in action, the hell-raising, irresponsible solider who can outfight anyone, on or off the battlefield. It is, of course, an exaggerated picture, a cartoon, but like the best cartoons, it only over-emphasises basic truths.

It is no exaggeration to say that the nation of Australia was founded on the way its men volunteered to fight before it was a nation, in New Zealand, in the flat and dehydrating heat of the Sudan, in the bleakness of a north Chinese winter, and in South Africa, the distant land so like their nation's home.

Awarded the VC for rescuing a mate, John Bisdee receives a warm welcome home from friends and well-wishers. Australia had marched into the 20th century an eager defender of the British Empire, but its fighting men had already demonstrated the spirit of a young, independent nation.

BIBLIOGRAPHY

Atkinson, J.J. *Australian Contingents To The China Field Force.* Sydney: The Clarendon Press, 1976.

Barthorp, Michael. *The Armies of Britain, 1485-1980.* London: The National Army Museum. n.d.

——. *To Fight the Daring Maoris.* London: Hodder & Stoughton, 1979.

Bartlett, Norman. ed. *Australia at Arms.* Canberra: Australian War Memorial, 1955.

Brereton, J.M. *A Guide to the Regiments & Corps of the British Army.* London: The Bodley Head Ltd., 1985.

Bruce, George. *Harbottle's Dictionary of Battles.* London: Granada Publishers, Ltd., 1979.

Buchan, John. *Memory Hold-the-Door.* London: Hodder & Stoughton, 1940.

Burleigh, Bennett. *The Natal Campaign.* 1900.

Carman, W.Y. *A Dictionary of Military Uniform.* New York: Scribner, 1977.

Chamberlain, M. *To Shoot & Ride.* 1967.

Churchill, Winston. *My Early Life.* London: Macmillan, 1941.

——. *Great Contemporaries.* London: Butterworth, 1938.

Cutlack, F.M. *Breaker Morant.* Sydney: Ure Smith Pty. Ltd., 1962.

Denton, Kit. *Closed File.* Adelaide: Rigby Publishing, 1983.

Doyle, Arthur Conan. *The Great Boer War.* London: Bell, 1900.

Dupuy, R.E. & T.N. *The Encyclopedia of Military History.* London: MacDonald & Co. (Publishers) Ltd., 1977.

Firkins, Peter. *The Australians in Nine Wars.* Sydney: Pan Books, 1972.

Griffith, Kenneth. *Thank God We Kept the Flag Flying.* London: Hutchinson, 1974.

Harrison, David. *The White Tribe of Africa.* London: British Broadcasting Corporation, 1985.

Hobson, J.A. *The War in South Africa, its Causes and Effects.* London: 1900.

King, R.E. *The Boer War, 1889-1900.* London: R.E. King, 1900.

Kruger, Rayne. *Goodbye Dolly Gray.* London: New English Library Ltd., 1959.

Laffin, John. *Digger: The Legend of the Australian Soldier.* Melbourne: Macmillan & Co., 1986.

Larkins, W.R. & Lord Loch. *A Short Account of Loch's Horse 1902-3* private papers.

Lee, Emanoel. *To The Bitter End.* London: Penguin Books, Ltd., 1985.

MacDonald, John. *Great Battlefields of the World.* London: Joseph, 1984.

Macksey, Kenneth. *The History of Land Warfare.* New York: Guinness Superlatives, Ltd., 1973.

Messenger, Charles. *A History of the British Army.* London: Bison Books, 1986.

Mitchell, Elyne. *Light Horse.* Melbourne: Sun, 1978.

Montague, Ronald. *Dress and insignia of the British Army in Australia & New Zealand, 1770-1870.* Sydney: Library of Australian History, 1981.

Montgomery of Alamein, *A History of Warfare.* London: William Collins, Sons & Co. Ltd., 1968.

Morris, James. *Heaven's Command.* London: Faber and Faber, 1973.

——. *Pax Britannica.* London: Faber and Faber, 1979.

——. *Farewell the Trumpets.* London: Faber and Faber, 1978.

Nicholls, Bob. *Blue Jackets & Boxers.* Sydney: Allen & Unwin, 1986.

Pakenham, Thomas. *The Boer War.* London: Weidenfeld & Nicolson Ltd., 1979.

Palmer, Roy. *The Rambling Soldier.* Middlesex: Penguin Books, 1977.

Paterson, A.B. *Happy Despatches.* Sydney: Lansdowne Press, 1980.

Pearl. Cyril. *Morrison of Peking.* Sydney: Angus & Robertson, 1967.

Pemberton, W. Baring. *Battles of the Boer War.* London: Pan Books, 1969.

Reitz, Denys. *Commando.* Middlesex: Penguin Books, 1948.

Rogers, Col. H.C.B. *Weapons of the British Soldier.* Great Britain: Sphere Books, 1972.

Schulenberg, C.A.R. "Die Buishveldt Carbineers", *Historika,* Official Journal of the South African Society, 1981.

Semmler, Dr. Clement. *The Banjo of the Bush.* Melbourne: Lansdowne Press, 1975.

Stanley, Peter (ed.) *But Little Glory.* Canberra: Military Historical Society of Australia, 1985.

Tuchman, Barbara W. *The Proud Tower.* New York: Macmillan, 1966.

Wallace, Edgar. *Unofficial Dispatches.* London: Hutchinson & Co., 1901.

Wallace, R.L. *The Australians at the Boer War.* Canberra: Australian War Memorial and the Government Publishing Service, 1976.

Wedd, Monty. *Australian Military Uniforms, 1800-1982.* Kenthurst: Kangaroo Press, 1982.

Wilkinson Latham, John. *British Military Swords, 1800 to the Present Day.* New York: Crown Publishers, 1967.

Wilkinson Latham, Robert & Christopher. *Infantry Uniforms, 1855-1939.* London: Blandford Press, 1970.

Witton, G.C. *Scapegoats of the Empire.* Sydney: Angus & Robertson, 1982.

ACKNOWLEDGMENTS

For their help in the preparation of this book, the author and publishers wish to thank the staff of the Australian War Memorial, Canberra, especially Dr Michael McKernan, George Imashev, Andrew Jack, Beryl Strusz. We would also like to thank Mihri Tansley, Peter Huck, Charles Goodwin, Jan Bassett, Mrs Perdita McCarthy, Leanne Collins, Max Chamberlain, Chris Coulthard-Clark, Warrant Officer Ian Kuring, Royal Australian Infantry Corps Museum, Singleton, NSW, Jemmy Ghobrial, Flexigraphics, the United Service Institution of NSW, Roger Scott, Bob Leonard, Westpac, and David Lempriere.

PICTURE CREDITS

Credits from left to right are separated by semicolons, from top to bottom by oblique strokes. AWM = Australian War Memorial.

COVER and page 1: AWM P187/07/06.

FROM BRITISH BEGINNINGS. 6-9: State Library. 10, 11: Mitchell Library. 12, 13: State Library.

UNDER THE SOUTHERN CROSS. 14: Drawing by Charles Goodwin. 16, 17: Map by Flexigraphics. 18: Mitchell Library. 19: Author's collection. 20: Hocken Library, University of Otago. 22, 23: The Picturesque Atlas of Australasia. 24: National Library of Australia. 26: Mitchell Library. 27: Map by Flexigraphics. 29: B5592 State Library of South Australia. 30: Alexander Turnbull Library, NZ. 31: National Library of Australia.

SWORD AND BRUSH. 33: National Library of Australia. 34-37: Alexander Turnbull Library (Paul Hamlyn Collection). 38: Alexander Turnbull Library / AWM 19817. 39, 40: Alexander Turnbull Library. 41: National Library of Australia / AWM 50018.

AFRICA AT ARMS. 42: Drawings by Charles Goodwin. 44: Picture supplied by Military Archives & Research Services, Lincs. (National Portrait Gallery, London) / AWM 19552. 45: Map by Flexigraphics. 46, 47: National Library of Australia. 48, 49: AWM A3999. 51: AWM 4941. 52: AWM A4732 / AWM 3 DRL 6504. 53: National Library of Australia.

SUDAN EXPEDITION. 54, 55: State Library of NSW. 56, 57: AWM A 5138; AWM A5137. 58, 59: Mitchell Library; AWM P441/01 / AWM A4402.

A SAILOR'S CAMPAIGN. 60: Drawing by Charles Goodwin. 62: Maps by Flexigraphics. 63: Courtesy United Services Institution of NSW (USI). 64: AWM A4807. 65: Courtesy USI. 66: AWM A5042. 67: AWM P417/37/14. 69: Courtesy USI. 70: Courtesy USI / AWM A4935. 71: Courtesy USI. 73: Courtesy USI / AWM P417/37/14. 74: AWM A5050.

THE ELUSIVE BOER. 76, 77: AWM A4925. 78, 79: AWM A4917. 79: Courtesy USI. 80, 81: AWM A4933 / AWM P93/13/07; Courtesy USI. 82: AWM A4341. 83: Courtesy USI. 84, 85: Print supplied by MARS (Roger Viollet, Paris).

THE TREK TO WAR. 86: Drawing by Charles Goodwin. 88: Maps by Flexigraphics. 90, 91: Courtesy USI. 92: Author's collection. 93: Courtesy USI. 94: National Army Museum, Chelsea. 95: B8828 State Library of South Australia. 96, 97: Courtesy USI / AWM A4930. 98: Print supplied by MARS (Personality Pictures Library). 99: AWM P492/06/06. 100-105 Courtesy USI. 106: AWM P413/52/11.

LIFE ON THE VELDT. 108, 109: Courtesy USI. 110: AWM A4292. 111: Courtesy USI. 112: Courtesy USI. 113: AWM A4438. 114, 115: Courtesy USI. 116, 117: AWM P422/20/05.

ROBERTS TAKES THE REINS. 118: Drawing by Charles Goodwin. 120, 121: AWM A4416. 122: Map by Flexigraphics. 124: National Library of Australia. 125: Courtesy USI. 126: AWM A5168. 129: Courtesy USI. 133: AWM A4919. 135: AWM A1189. 137: AWM A4792. 138, 139: Courtesy USI. 140: AWM A5079. 142, 143: AWM A5076.

FROM REDCOAT TO KHAKI. 145: Drawing by Charles Goodwin. 146, 147: AWM 19713; Drawing by Charles Goodwin. 148: Drawing by Charles Goodwin. 150, 151: AWM 19564. 152: AWM 19505. 153: AWM 19794.03.

ENDGAME. 154: Drawing by Charles Goodwin. 156, 157: Courtesy USI. 158, 159: AWM A5311; AWM A5815 / AWM A5828; AWM A5815. 161: National Library of Australia. 163: AWM A4425.

Every effort has been made to contact and acknowledge owners of copyright in illustrative material used in this book. In the case of an ommission, holders of copyright are invited to contact:
    John Ferguson Publishers
    100 Kippax St.
    Surry Hills, N.S.W.
    2010.

INDEX

Numerals in italics indicate an illustration of the subject mentioned.

A
Abbott, Corporal J.H.M., 110
Angas, G.F., 34, 35
Arab, troopship, 53
Argus, newspaper, 28
Ashanti, 96
Atcherly, Henry Mount Langton, 36, 38, 39
Auckland, 21, 22, *map* 27, 28
Auckland Rifle Volunteers, 28, 31
Australasian, troopship, 46
Australian Commonwealth Horse, 154, 162
Avon HMS, 29

B
Baden-Powell, Colonel R.S.S., at Mafeking, 96-97; *97,* 118, 132, at Elands River relief, 134, 138
Basutoland, 87 *map* 88, *map* 122
Bay of Islands, 21, 22, *map* 27
Beatson, Major-General S.B., 160
Bell, Lieutenant Frederick, VC, 135, 137
Belmont Station, *map* 88, 98, *map* 122, 136
Bisdee, Trooper John, VC, 135, 137, *163*
Black Cuffs, the, 19, 22, 149, *see also* Regiments: 58th of Foot
Black Week, 92, 107, 118-119
Bloemfontein, *map* 88, 93, 97, Banjo Paterson at, 102; 119-120, *map* 122, 124-125, 128, 130-131, 136, 142, 144, protected area around, 155
Boer, 17, 18, 64, *78-85, 81,* in South Africa to brink of war, 86-89, 92-94; lack of fair play, 99; *100,* at Modder River and Magersfontein, 103-106; *105,* 107, at Sunnyside Kopje and Spion Kop, 118-120; besieged at Paardeberg, 123-125; de Wet's commando, 128-130; Botha's forces 132-134; at Elands River, 138-142; decline of forces, 154-157; Pretoria peace conference, 162-163
Boer War, 15, 61, 86, First Boer War (1880-1881), 89; *90,* outbreak of Second Boer War (1889), 94-95; the press, 102; nurses, 130; Australian VC's 135; Australian unit actions, 136-137; 149, weapons at, 153; 159, end of, 162
Botha, Louis, *83,* at Colenso, 106-107; 128, at Klip River and Diamond Hill, 132-133; 136, 141, meeting with Kitchener, 160; *161,* 162
Bothaville, *map* 122, 137, 144
Boxers, the, 60-63, *69-71,* 72-74
Boxer Rebellion, 62
Bridge, Major Cyprian, 22, 24, 33, 36, 38, 41
British Army, 8, 15, 17, 18, 28, 32, 78, 145
British Empire, 8, *map* 16-17, 18, 43, 46, 47, 60, 87, 94, 142, 156-157, 163
British South Africa Company, 92, 98
Broadwood, Colonel R.C., 130-131
Bruce, Rear Admiral J.A.T., 63
Bulawayo, *114,* 130
Buller, General Sir Redvers, *92,* 95-98, at Colenso, 105-107; in Natal and at Spion Kop, 119-120; 123, relief of Ladysmith, 127; departure, 128; 139
Bush Veldt Carbineers, 158-159, 160

C
Camel Corps, Sudan, 52, *58*
Cameron, Major-General Duncan, 26-28, 30, 31
Cape Colony, 87, *map* 88, 89, 92-93, 97-98, 118, *map* 122, 130, 160
Cape of Good Hope, 86, 87, *map* 88
Cape Town, *map* 88, 95, 131
Carey, Brigadier-General, 31
Chang-wang Fu palace, 74
Chief Kawiti, 23, 24
China Field Force, 68
Chronicle, the, San Francisco, 75
Churchill, Winston, in Sudan 50; 102, at Spion Kop, 123; 131
Clarke, Captain A.C., 67
Colenso, *map* 88, 92, 97, 106-107, *map* 122, 136
Colley, General Sir George, 89
Concentration camps, 140, 155-156
Cook, Captain James, 18-20, 35
Cox, Captain Charles, 95
Crimean War, 14-15, 26, 50, 102, 123, 135
Cronje, General Piet, 94, 96, 99, 101, at Magersfontein, 104; at Paardeberg, 123-124; 129, 136

D
Dalley, William Bede, (acting Premier, NSW), 45
De Aar, *map* 88, 97, *map* 122
De Beers Consolidated Mines, 98
De la Rey, Koos, 99, 107, 120, at Elands River, 134; 136-137, 138, 141, 151, 161, 162
Dervishes, 42-43, 45, 49, *51*
De Wet, General Christiaan, *81,* 120, at Paardeberg, 126-127; 128, at Sannah's Post, 130-131; 133, *133,* 135, 137, at Elands River, 138; *138-139,* 141, 144, 154, 157, 160-162
Diamond Hill, *map* 122, 133, 136, 142
Digna, Osman, 42, 50, 51
Doyle, Arthur Conan, 123
Drakensberg Mountains, *map* 88, 89, 94
Dreifontein Kopjes, *map* 122, 128
Dundonald, Lord, 107
Durban, *map* 88, 97, *map* 122
Dutch East India Company, 20, 86

E
Elandslaagte, *map* 88, 94
Elands River Post, 97, *map* 122, 133-134, 136, 139, 142
El Obeid, 42, *map* 45
El Teb, 43, *map* 45
Eureka Stockade, 8, *11,* 15

F
Fawcett, Millicent, 140
Flagstaff Hill, Battle of, 22
Forest Rangers, 31, 36, *36, 39,* 40
Fraser, Sergeant R.D., *152*
French, Major-General Sir John, 120, at Klip Drift and Paardeberg, 123-124; 160

G
Gallipoli, 15, 18, 135, 162
Ganges, hospital ship, 52
Gatacre, Major-General Sir William, 98, defeat at Stormberg, 103
Gilfillan, J.A., 34, 35
Gilfillan, Corporal J.R., 110
Gill, Samuel, 7
Gladstone, Prime Minister William Ewart, 43, 45
Gordon, General Charles "Chinese", 43, 44, *44,* 45, 49
Gore-Brown, Governor Thomas, 25, 26
Graham, Major-General Sir Gerald, 50
"Grand Canal", China, 68
Graspan, *map* 122, 136
Great Trek, the, 87
Great War, the, 14, 18, 93
Grey, Sir George, 26

H
Hai Ho River, *map* 62, 63, 68
Hales, A.G., 119
Hamilton, Major-General Ian, 131-133

Hammond, Charles 150-151
Handcock, Sergeant Peter, 158-159, *158-159*, 160
Hart, Major-General Fitzroy, 107, 127
Hau Haus, 32, 36
Hazard, HMS, 21-24
Heese, Dr., 158
Henderson, J.B., 11
Herford, Captain Walter, 31
Her Majesty Queen Victoria, 7, 18, *18,* 45, 75, 112, 135, 144
Hertzog, Judge, 162
Hicks, General William, 42
Hildyard, Major-General Henry, 107
Hlangwane Hill, 106-107, *map* 122
Hobhouse, Emily, 140
Hobson, Captain William, 20, *20,* 21
Hone Heke Pokai, 21-22, *22,* 23-24
Hore, Colonel, 134, 138
Howse, Lieutenant Neville, VC, 128, 135, 136
Hulme, Lieutenant-Colonel William, 22-24
Hunt, Captain Frederick, 158, *158-159*
Hutt Valley, 22, *map* 27

I
Iberia, troopship, 46
Imperial Light Horse, 96, 127
Indian Mutiny, 15, 126
Isandhlawana, 89

J
Jackson, Captain William, 31
Jameson, Dr. Leander Starr, 92, 98
Joubert, General Piet, at Laing's Nek, 89; 93, *93,* against White's Natal Defence Corps, 94, 96
Johannesburg, *map* 88, 92, 96, *map* 122, 132-133, 136

K
Kalifa Abdullah, 51
Karri-Davies, Walter, 96
Kate, schooner, 27
Kekewich, Lieutenant Colonel Robert, 98
Kendall, Thomas, 19
Khartoum, 43, 44, *map* 45, 49, 51, 119
Kimberley, *map* 88, 89, 94, 96-99, 104-105, 107, 119-120, *map* 122, 123-124, 128, 129, 136
Kingdom of Kush, 42
King Movement, the, 25, 26
Kitchener, Lord, in Sudan, 51; arrives in South Africa, 119-120; 123, *124,* at Paardeberg, 127; in Bloemfontein, 128; 133, 137; at Elands River, 138; 140, 142, 144, 151, land-clearing "drives", 154-157; peace meeting with Botha, 160; *161*
Klerksdorp, *150-151*
Klip Drift, *map* 122, 123
Knox, Major-General Charles, 144
Koheroa, 26, 27
Kororareka, 21, 22, *map* 27
Kroonstad, *map* 122, 132
Kruger, Paul (Oom Paul), 87, 89, move to independence, 92-94; *94,* left for Europe, 133; 137, 144

L
Ladysmith, *map* 88, 92, 94, 96-97, 105-107, 120, *map* 122, 127, 128
Lake Omapere, 23, *map* 27
Laing's Nek, *map* 88, 89, 94
Learoyd, Private William, 50, *52*
Lempriere, Sister Janey, *131*
Lenehan, Major Robert, 159
Lloyd George, 140-142, 155
Loch, Lord, 118
Lofts, Lieutenant H.E., *64,* 66
Loftus, Governor Lord, 47
London Gazette, the, 135
Long, Colonel C.J., 107
Lyne, Sir William, 64
Lyon-Fremantle, Major-General A.J., 50

M
Mafeking, *map* 88, 92, 94, 96, *96,* 97-98, 100, 107, 109, *map* 122, 132-133, 134, 136, 138, 140, 159, 161
Magersfontein, *map* 88, 92, 104-105, 107, *map* 122, 123, 129, 136
Mahdi, 42-45, 50, 51
Mahon, Colonel Bryan, 97, 132
Maiki Hill, 21-22
Majuba Hill, First Boer War, 89; 93, 127, 128
Maoris, 19-32, *34-35,* 35-36, *37, 39,* prisoners, 41; 162
Matabele, 89, 98
Matson, Captain H., 19, 22
Maxim machine-gun, 15, 67, 78, *79,* 104, 134, 137, *153*
Maygar, Lieutenant Leslie, VC, 135, 137
Meremere, 26, *map* 27
Methuen, Lieutenant-General Lord, Kimberley relief force, 97-99; defeat at Modder River and Magersfontein, 103-105; 123-124, 161
Middelburg, *map* 88, 160
Milner, Sir Alfred, 93
Modder River, *map* 88, 99, 103, 120, *map* 122, 123, 126, 136, bridge, *140*
Morant, Harry Harbord, "The Breaker", 102, 130, *158-159,* 160
Morris, Major, 160
Morrison, George "Chinese", 73, *73*
Mount Egmont, 25, *map* 27

N
Natal, 15, *map* 88, 89, *90,* 98, 106, 118-120, *map* 122, 123, 127, 130, 132, 139
Natal Carbineers, 127
Natal Defence Force, 94
New Zealand Company, 20, 25
Nile River, 43, 44, *map* 45, 49, 51
Nixon, E., nurse, 130
Norman, Lieutenant Thomas, 30
North Island, New Zealand, *map* 27, 35
North China Daily News, 69
North Star, HMS, 19

O
Omdurman, 50, 51, 119
Orakau, *map* 27, 31
Orange Free State, 87, *map* 88, 89, 93, 94, 96, *map* 122, 123, 128, 130, 132-133, 139, 144, 154, 160-162
Orange River, 87, *map* 88, 89, 99, 103, *map* 122, *132,* 160
Ottoshoop, *map* 122, 137

P
Paardeberg, *map* 122, 126, 136
Pao-ting Fu, 72
Papatoetoe, *map* 27, 28
Parkes, Sir Henry, 46, 47
Parkinson, Sydney, 35
Patea River, 25, *map* 27
Paterson, Andrew Barton, "Banjo", 102-103, 128
Pei Ho River, 63,
Pei Tang, *map* 62, 68
Peking, *map* 62, 65, 68-69, 72-73, *73,* 74-75
Perceval, Lieutenant John, 30
Picton, Harry, 158, *158-159*
Pietersburg, 137, 158
Pilcher, Colonel T.D., 119
Pioneer, HMS, 29
Plumer, Lieutenant-Colonel Sir Herbert, 96, 109, 132
Potatau Te Wherowhero (King Potatau I), 25
Pratt, Major-General Thomas, 26
Pretoria, 77, *85, map* 88, 120, *map* 122, 130-134, 136, 139, 142, 144, 161
Pretorius, Marthinus, 87

Prinsloo, Commandant Martin, 133
Protector HMCS, 64, 66
Puketutu, 23, *map 27*

Q
Queensland Mounted Infantry, 119, 131, 134

R
Rangariri, 26-30, *map 27, 30*
Regiments: 58th of Foot (Rutlandshire), 14, 18, 19, 22, 23, *33, 38, 145, 147,* 162; 96th, 21-22; 12th of Foot, 26; Suffolk, 26, 29; 14th (West Yorkshires), 26, 29; 70th (Surrey), 28; 1st Waikato Militia, 28, 36, 38, *39;* 2nd Waikato Militia, 28; 3rd Waikato Militia, 28; 4th Waikato Militia, 28; 40th (Somersetshires), 29, 30; 18th (Royal Irish), 31; 15th (Sikh), 49-50; Bengal Cavalry, 49-50; Indian Lancers, 50; Coldstream, 49-50; Grenadier, 49-50; Scots, 49; Berkshire, 49-50; NSW Lancers, 95, 98, 102-103, 119-120, 128; 6th Inniskilling Dragoons, 95, 120; Black Watch, 105; Seaforth Highlanders, 105; Argylls, 105; Highland Light Infantry, 105; Protectorate, 96; 11th of Foot (North Devon), 9; 21st Lancers, 51; Wei-hai-wei, 68
Reit River, *map 88, map 122,* 123
Rewi, Waikato Chief, 31-32
Rhodes, Cecil, 89, 92, 98, *98,* 124, 161
Roberts, Field Marshal Lord, 92, 107, 118-120, 123, 124, *126,* 127, 128-130, 132-134, 139, 141-142, 144, 155
Roberts, Tom, 152
Robley, Major-General Horatio Gordon, 36, 41
Rogers, Sergeant James, VC, 135, 137
Rorke's Drift, map 88, 89
Rowell, Lieutenant Peter, 133
Royal Horse Artillery, 49-50, 103, 130
Royal Marines, 18, 21, *49,* 68, 98
Royal Navy, 64, 66, 67, 68, 158
Royal Red Cross, 130
Ruapekapeka, *33, 41*
Russell, Captain, 22

S
Salamis, S.S., 64, 66, *66,* 68
Sannah's Post, 130
Seymour, Vice Admiral Sir Edward, 62, 63
Slingersfontein, 119, *120-121, map* 122, 136
Smuts, Jan, *83,* 93, 137, 140, 141, 160, 162
Society of Righteous and Harmonious Fists (I-ho-ch'uan), 61, 63, 69, *see also* Boxers
South Africa, 17, 18, 44, 61, 63, 64, 75, 86-87, *map 88,* 89, 92-96, 102, 105, 107, 110–112, 122, *map 122,* 128, 130, 133, 135, 137, 139, 140, 144, 149, 153, 155, 157, 159, 161-162
South African Republic, 87, 89, 93
South Australian Volunteer Forces 29
Spion Kop, 120, *map 122,* 123, *125,* 127
Star of India, troopship, 27
Steyn, Marthinus, 93, 94, 133, 144, 161
Stormberg, *map 88,* 92, 103, 107, *map 122,* 136
Suakin, 43, 45, *47,* 49, 50, 52, *59*
Sudan, the, 17, 42-52, *map 45,* 55, 56, 58-59, 119, 146-147, 149, rifle used in, 153
Sunnyside Kopje, 118, *map 122,* 136
Sydney Mail, the, 46, 47
Sydney Morning Herald, the, 28, 50, 74, 102, 128

T
Taku, *map 62,* 63, forts at, *65;* 68
Talana Hill, *map 88,* 94
Tamai, *map 45, 49,* 50, *51,* 52
Tamaikowha, Maori rebel leader, 39
Tamati Waka Nene (Timothy Walker), 20, *20, 22,* 22
Taranaki, 25, 32, 37
Tasman, Abel, 19
Tawhiao (King), 25, 30
Thomas, Major James Francis, *159, 159,* 160
The Times, 73, 102
Thompson, Captain, 22
Tientsin, *map 62,* 63, 68, 72, 74, 75
Transvaal, 87, *map 88,* 89, 92, 93, 94, *map 122,* 130, 132-133, 139, 154, 160-162

Treaty of Pretoria, 89
Treaty of Waitangi, 20, 21, 23, 25
Tugela River, *map 88,* 97, 106, 120, *map 122, 125,* 127
Tzu Hsi (Dowager Empress), 61, 62, 63, 69, 73

V
Vaal Kranz, 123, 127
Vaal River, 87, *map 88,* 97, 119, *map 122,* 131, 136, 161
Valsch River, 144
Vereeniging, 161
Velocity, transport, 19
Victoria Barracks, *56,* 64
Victoria Cross, 92, 96, 107, 124, 129, 135-137, 163
Victoria HMS, 26
Von Kettler, Baron, 73
Von Tempsky, Captain Gustavus, 31, *31,* 36-37, *37,* 39, *40*

W
Waikare Lake, 27, *map 27*
Waikato (King Country), 24
Waikato River, 26, 27, *map 27,* 29
Waitangi, 20, 23, *map 27*
Waitara River, 25, *map 27*
Wallace, Edgar, 102
Watkins, Kennet, 40
Wauchope, Major-General Andrew, 104-105
Weir, Private Robert, 52, *59*
Wentworth, William Charles, 25
White, General Sir George, besieged in Ladysmith, 94, 96, 106-107, 127; 128
Williams, Lieutenant-Colonel E.A., 38
Wiremu Kingi (William King), 24, 25
Wiremu Tamihana, 30
Witton, George, 158
Witwatersrand (the Rand), *map 88,* 89, *map 122,* 132, 136
Wolfe, General, 18
Wylly, Lieutenant Guy, VC, 135, 137
Wynyard, Lieutenant-Colonel R.H., 19

Z
Zand River, *map 122,* 136, *142-143*
Zulu (amaZulu), 87, 89, 96
Zululand, *map 88,* 89
Zulu War, 89, 92